Marian Tracy's Complete Chicken Cookery

Marian Tracy's
COMPLETE
CHICKEN COOKERY

by Marian Tracy

Illustrated by

MARGUERITE BURGESS

THE BOBBS-MERRILL COMPANY, INC.
PUBLISHERS

INDIANAPOLIS   NEW YORK

First Edition

TO
IRMA S. ROMBAUER
WITH MUCH LOVE
AND ADMIRATION

East Indian Chicken

1 frying chicken, quartered
  Salt and pepper
5 tablespoons butter
2 cups orange juice
¼ cup finely chopped onion
½ teaspoon salt
1 tablespoon curry powder
1 tablespoon flour

Sprinkle chicken with salt and pepper. Melt butter in skillet; brown chicken on both sides. Add ½ cup orange juice and onion; cover and cook 10 minutes, spooning juice over chicken occasionally. Mix together ½ teaspoon salt and curry powder; add 2 tablespoons orange juice and mix until smooth. Pour over chicken; cover and cook 25 to 30 minutes, cr until tender, basting occasionally.

Remove chicken to warm platter. Gradually stir 2 tablespoons orange juice into flour; mix until smooth. Stir in (Continued on Page 46)

fres

Real tea refreshment—
Hot or iced, new Li
you fresh-brewed fl
full-bodied, refreshir
stant. Instantly, delic

Dissolves instantly...
Anyone can make ne
any time. Just spoon c
instantly you get the
fer. Never too weak, n
perfect. So economic
1½ cents per serving.

Hot or iced, it

A precise blend of choice teas flavor-protected

Introduction

Chicken is the most accommodating of all birds, even of all meats, using that term loosely. Dishes range all the way from a Coq au Vin prepared skillfully and lengthily and lovingly for a festive dinner to a simple chicken-and-corn casserole hastily but intelligently concocted from a couple of cans.

The flavor is gentle and amenable, blending equally well with lots of sweet butter in the bland, artful and implausible dish that is known as Cotelette Kiev or with a hot fiery barbecue sauce.

In its many guises chicken delights the sophisticates and satisfies simple tastes and robust appetites. Roasted crisply or boiled, it soothes the pangs of ulcer victims and is pleasing and fit for the very old and the very young. It is a party dish, an everyday dish, a light dish, a sturdy dish—it's a picnic dish, goes to school or to work in lunch boxes, and is ubiquitous at weddings in salads or patties. Gently cooked and smelling somewhat aromatically of brandy, the hot chicken livers accompany the cocktails. The fat carefully hoarded from plump and mature hens is plain heavenly in almost any kind of cooking, especially baking. Broth saved from boiling or stewing a hen embellishes sauces, soups, gravies and casseroles.

These days there *is* a chicken in almost every pot (and Henry IV of France said that long, long, before our politicians)—and why not? It's plentiful, comparatively inexpensive and available almost any way one wishes. Whole chickens may be bought fresh or frozen and range in size from broilers to roasters to stewing hens or fowls, and to the aristocrats of them all, the pampered, plump, pallid and celibate capons usually roasted. Chicken may be bought fresh or frozen in parts—breasts, drumsticks, second joints or thighs as they are genteelly called on the box, wings, backs, hearts, livers, gizzards and so on, though at this moment I can't think of anything else. Canned it is available whole or half in gravy—with or without giblets—fricasseed, boned, à la king, cream soup, broth, fat and probably by the time this book gets in the stores still other ways.

In this book there are basic rules for cooking chicken and many, many short cuts. Recipes for some dishes are complex, elaborate and somewhat lengthy; many are streamlined. My time, my energy, my inclinations and the occasion vary from day to day as must anyone's. Most of the long ways of doing things are the best but not always feasible or even possible.

I have no fixed convictions about the flavor of fresh chicken versus the flavor of frozen. Undoubtedly the finest fresh chicken, freshly killed, would be the best, but in the city I don't have that, so usually I use frozen parts in which the quality is controlled. They may be kept on hand and are so wonderfully convenient to use for meals for one, or two, or three, or four. The whole chickens I buy fresh, partly because in a city apartment there is not room to store them in the refrigerator freezer, and partly because it takes too long for rigor mortis to pass off. It is the drawback to frozen chicken. The best way is to let it thaw gradually in the regular part of the refrigerator. The next best, and faster, way is at room temperature. Not recommended but often necessary in a hurry is the shameful practice of putting the frozen chicken, outside carton removed, but still in the cellophane covering, into a pan of lukewarm water.

All chickens fresh or frozen taste best and are apt to be tenderest when brought to room temperature before cooking. This is particularly true of the livers. The amounts and the times given in this book for whole chicken are for what is called ready-to-cook, which sounds more expensive per pound than dressed but which ends up about the same amount per edible pound and is more convenient to use.

The basic ways of cooking chicken are few. They may be roasted, baked, stewed (boiled, poached, fricasseed), or broiled, barbecued, fried in deep fat or shallow, or cooked in casseroles. The variations are almost literally infinite and no book is, or ever will be, truly complete despite the title of this book. Some variations are minor—a lavish amount of pimientos in proportion to the chicken breasts makes a dish into something special, or some curry powder and crumbled bacon and white grapes added to an otherwise flat salad add zing and a fresh taste that delights on a very hot day. Chopped walnuts give a Mediterranean touch to sautéed and sauced chicken that pleases and does not shock conventional palates.

Roast chicken is wonderfully simple and wonderfully good done in an electric rotisserie. Place the chicken—well trussed, legs tied neatly behind the tail and wings folded back—on the spit according to specific directions, turn on the current and let the bird whirl around for the specified minutes per pound—an hour and one quarter to an hour and one half for most roasting-size chickens. By this method a crisp skin with a juicy tender flesh is achieved; it takes practically no skill, energy or preparation time. It is miraculous and well worth the price of the equipment. The meat may be used flavorfully in salads or any dishes requiring cooked meat. The broth you might have had if it had been boiled may be made in the meantime by simmering the giblets and neck in 2 or 3 cups of water with a slice of onion, a stalk of celery, salt and pepper and whatever other seasoning is pleasing. A roasting chicken (4 to 5½ lbs.) should take about 1½ hours and a 2½ to 3-lb. chicken ¾ hour. For a stuffed chicken add five minutes more. Do not store stuffed chickens either before or after cooking. Keep the stuffing separate. It can spoil and not be evident.

To roast a chicken in the oven, set the oven control at 325° to 350°—no more. A chicken 2½ to 3½ lbs. will take about 1 hour; a 4 to 5-lb. chicken will take 1½ to 2 hours. Roast the well-buttered chicken in an open pan; allow slightly more time when the bird is stuffed. The bird is done when the flesh is slightly shrunken beneath the brown crisp skin and the thick portion of the breast and thighs is tender and does not drip a pink juice when speared carefully with a fork or skewer, and when the joints aren't stiff when worked gently with the fingers, which are well protected, naturally, with a towel.

Frying is only, of course, for young chickens, 2½ to 3 lbs., ready-to-cook. As anyone knows who has read even four recipes for fried chicken, there are no two people who agree exactly. There are many ways given elsewhere in this book. But the simplest is to dust the pieces lightly with seasoned flour by shaking a few in a paper bag with the flour, and fry in a heavy skillet that has about ½ inch of fat in it. What fat to use is another contentious subject. Any may be used. I am apt to use olive oil, but that is a personal idiosyncrasy; part butter and part lard is good. Cook over a moderate flame, turning the pieces from time to time until golden brown. Then cover and cook over a very low flame until tender. Drain on paper towels and keep warm until ready to serve. The thickest pieces of a 2½-lb. chicken can be done usually in 20 to 25 minutes. To deep fry, flour the same way and cook in fat heated to 350°, 7 to 10 minutes for the small pieces, 8 to 14 minutes for the large. An electric fryer is a pleasure and a convenience. Chicken quartered and halved is cooked in fat 12 to 14 minutes. It is only fair to warn you that many like chicken deep fried and many don't.

Old hens or fowl, over 4½ lbs., are best cooked in moist heat, which means boiling, stewing, simmering or poaching—whatever you wish to call it. Put the chicken, whole or cut up, in a heavy kettle that has a tight-fitting lid. Add about 3 cups water and 2 teaspoons to 1 tablespoon salt, a small carrot, an onion, 2 or 3 stalks celery or some celery seeds, and 3 or 4 peppercorns. Bring the water to a boil; cover and turn the heat down very low. Simmer until the thickest pieces are tender when pierced with a fork, 2 hours or more, being careful that it does not boil at any time. If the chicken is to be used in a salad, it will be juicier if allowed to cool in the liquid. Otherwise take it out of the pot and strain the stock. Make a gravy according to any of the recipes in the book or save the stock for soups and sauces. A chicken may be stewed in a pressure pan more expeditiously, in fact, in 25 to 30 minutes at 10 lbs. pressure (15 lbs. if the pressure pan has only one gauge), but the long way is a little gentler.

In broiling use very young birds only. The heat is turned down to moderate and the broiler or pan with the birds skin side down and brushed with melted butter, salt and pepper, is placed 5 or 6 inches from the heat. Turn the pieces from time to time, basting all the while until tender.

Carving a chicken is not very complicated. The legs and the wings are cut off first, and the second joint and the leg separated, if desired, depending on the size of the chicken and the occasion. The breast is sliced lengthwise.

As in the writing of any specialty cook book this one became an obsession with friends eating chicken after chicken after chicken. In restaurants I saw nothing on menus but chicken. Some friends gave me recipes, others gave patience and understanding when it was needed. To these I am particularly grateful: Jessica McLaughlin, of the Wine Advisory Board, Pierre Ferro, Marcel Perret, Lynn Farnol, Jean Lapolla, Peg Sterling, Thelma Robard, Cynthia Watt, Bill Treadwell, Elisabeth Fairer, Muriel McCowey, and Fred Smith, of the Poultry and Egg National Board, who is in no way responsible for my interpretation of the material he gave me.

Marian Tracy

Contents

Marian Tracy's Complete Chicken Cookery

1

Boiled, Poached, Fricasseed and Stewed

BRUNSWICK STEW, No. 1

This rich Brunswick stew is better if prepared ahead of time and then reheated after "ripening."

> 4-lb. chicken, disjointed
> ¼ cup butter or bacon drippings
> ½ cup chopped onions
> 5 tomatoes, peeled and quartered (or
>   1 No. 2½ can)
> 6 cloves
>   Pepper
> 2 or 3 cups fresh or frozen lima beans
> 2 or 3 cups corn cut from the cob or
>   the canned whole-kernel corn
>   Salt
> 2 teaspoons Worcestershire sauce
> 1 cup toasted bread crumbs

Brown the chicken in the fat in a large, heavy pan or Dutch oven. Add the onions, tomatoes, 1 cup boiling water, cloves and pepper. Simmer together until the chicken is nearly tender, about 40 minutes. Then add the lima beans and corn. Simmer, covered, until tender. Season with salt, pepper and Worcestershire sauce. Stir in bread crumbs. This serves 8 normal appetites.

17

BASTARD BRUNSWICK STEW,
PRESSURE COOKED

The lima beans, potatoes and corn make this a Brunswick
stew. The curry powder, the pressure cooker and no
tomatoes make it a bastard one.

> 1 chicken (about 3 lbs.), cut up as for frying
> ¼ cup flour
> 1 tablespoon curry powder
> Salt and pepper
> 3 tablespoons fat, preferably bacon drippings
> 6 small potatoes, scraped
> 1 package frozen Fordhook lima beans
> 1 12-oz. can whole-kernel corn

Mix the flour, curry powder, salt and pepper together in
a paper bag and shake the pieces of chicken to coat lightly.
Brown the chicken in the fat in a skillet. Put the chicken
on a rack in the pressure cooker. Add the potatoes, beans
and ⅓ cup water. Cover and bring up to pressure. Cook 15
minutes at 10 lbs. pressure. Reduce pressure immediately according to instructions for your cooker. Add the
drained corn and any additional seasoning desired. Thick-
en juices if you like by mixing 1 tablespoon flour with 1
tablespoon water and stirring into the liquid and cooking
briefly until smooth and thickened. Serves 5 or 6.

BRUNSWICK STEW, No. 2

Best served with hush puppies, cole slaw and good bourbon. Like all other stews, it is variable but there must be lima beans, corn and tomatoes.

> 2 chickens (about 3 lbs. each)
> Corn cut from 6 large ears or 1 No. 2
>   can whole-kernel corn
> 5 medium-sized onions, chopped
> 1 lb. okra, sliced (not obligatory)
> 2 large green peppers, chopped
> 5 large ripe tomatoes, peeled and chopped,
>   or 1 No. 2½ can
> ½ lb. salt pork (lean)
> 2 lbs. lima beans, shelled, or
>   2 packages frozen lima beans
> 1 teaspoon Tabasco, or 1 pod red pepper
> Black pepper

Wash whole chickens, place in large pot, cover with water, add salt and bring to boil. Turn down heat so that pot just simmers. Cook, covered, for 1½ to 2 hours, until meat begins to separate from bones. Add all vegetables. Slice salt pork down to skin but not through it; add with vegetables. Add the seasonings.

Turn heat down again until stew barely simmers. Stir frequently so that stew does not stick to bottom. Taste, and add more seasonings if desired. In 2 to 2½ hours the stew will be a perfectly blended mixture of chicken meat and vegetables, of thick mushy consistency. Remove chicken bones and serve very hot. Serves about 10.

CHICKEN BREASTS POACHED IN CLAM BROTH

8 pieces chicken breasts
1 pint clam broth
3 tablespoons butter
3 tablespoons flour
Salt, pepper, dash of nutmeg

Put the chicken breasts in a pan with the clam broth and simmer over a low flame 50 minutes to 1 hour or until tender. Remove from the broth and keep warm. Melt the butter, blend in the flour and add the clam juice, stirring slowly until thickened and smooth. Pour over the chicken breasts and serve. Accompany perhaps by chopped spinach with sour cream and a bowl of small boiled new potatoes, served in their skins with chive butter and, naturally, a green salad. Serves 4.

CHICKEN CACCIATORE

A classic Italian dish much loved by Americans.

1 chicken (2½ to 3½ lbs.), cut up as for frying
½ cup olive oil
1 medium-sized onion, thinly sliced
3½ cups canned tomatoes (1 No. 2½ can
    or 8 medium-sized tomatoes)
1 clove garlic
Salt, pepper
½ cup white wine

Cook chicken in hot olive oil until delicately browned, turning it from time to time so that it browns evenly. Add onion and cook until onion is transparent and golden. Add tomatoes, garlic, salt and pepper. Cover and simmer until

chicken is tender and everything mingled, and simmer to
a rich, thick sauce, around 40 to 50 minutes. Add wine
last 15 minutes of cooking. Remove garlic clove before
serving. Serves 4 to 6.

CHICKEN FRICASSEE

1 ready-to-cook stewing chicken
    (about 3 lbs.), cut up as for frying
1 medium-sized onion, chopped
4 peppercorns, 2 cloves and small piece
    of bay leaf
1 tablespoon salt
3 tablespoons chicken fat
7 tablespoons flour
3 cups chicken broth
½ teaspoon grated lemon rind
¼ teaspoon black pepper
2 to 3 tablespoons white wine
1 egg yolk
¼ cup cream

Put the chicken in a large pot and just cover with boiling
water. Add onion, peppercorns, cloves, bay leaf and salt.
Simmer until meat is tender, about 2½ to 3 hours. Take
out the chicken and strain the broth. Make fricassee
gravy: Mix chicken fat and flour in a saucepan. Add 3
cups of the broth and cook, stirring constantly, until
thickened. Add lemon rind, pepper and white wine.

Check seasoning and add more to suit taste. Simmer for
about 5 minutes. Add chicken to the gravy and heat. Beat
egg yolk and cream together and add a little of the hot
gravy, stirring until blended. Pour into the chicken and
gravy mixture and cook for 2 or 3 minutes, stirring all
the while. Serve at once. Makes 5 to 6 servings.

CHICKEN SAUTÉ BARCELONA

1 chicken (about 3½ lbs.), cut up for frying
2 tablespoons butter or margarine
2 tablespoons salad oil
3 tablespoons flour
1 10-oz. can condensed consommé
½ cup California Burgundy or claret wine
½ cup sliced pimiento-stuffed olives
1 4-oz. can mushroom stems and pieces,
    drained
2 tablespoons minced onion
Salt and pepper

Brown the chicken in a mixture of the butter and salad oil. Remove chicken and drain. Add the flour to the drippings and blend well. Add the consommé and wine and cook, stirring, until it boils and thickens. Add remaining ingredients, and salt and pepper to taste. Return chicken to the sauce. Cover and simmer slowly about 45 minutes, or until tender, basting occasionally. Serves 3 or 4.

CHICKEN IN RED WINE

4 tablespoons bacon drippings or other fat
1 stewing chicken (4 to 5 lbs.), cut in
    pieces for serving
1 cup chicken broth (canned or
    bouillon-cube broth may be used)
1 8-oz. can tomato sauce
½ cup California Burgundy or other
    red table wine
1 medium-sized onion, thinly sliced
2 stalks celery, chopped
2 tablespoons parsley, chopped
    Salt and pepper to taste
6 medium-sized carrots, scraped and sliced
1 cup fresh or frozen peas, cooked
⅓ cup flour
2 tablespoons California sherry wine

Heat bacon drippings in a Dutch oven or other heavy kettle; add chicken and sauté until nicely browned on all sides. Add chicken broth, tomato sauce, Burgundy, onion, celery, parsley, salt and pepper. Bring to a boil, then cover and simmer gently for 2 to 2½ hours (or longer, if necessary), until chicken is almost tender. Add carrots; continue cooking for ½ hour, or until chicken and carrots are tender. Remove chicken and vegetables from liquid. Pour liquid into a measuring pitcher or bowl, skim off excess fat, add water to make 3 cups, return to Dutch oven. Heat to boiling; mix flour and the ⅔ cup water to a smooth paste. Add slowly to the boiling liquid, stirring constantly. Simmer for 5 minutes or so. Season to taste with salt and pepper. Add sherry. Return chicken and vegetables to gravy. Add peas. Heat thoroughly before serving. Serves 5 or 6.

CHICKEN STEW WITH GARBANZOS

Garbanzos, chick-peas or *ceci,* whatever you wish to call them, are becoming available in more and more places and are a flavorful, nutty alternative to the more usual rice, potatoes and *pasta.*

> 1 clove garlic, peeled and cut in half
> ¼ cup olive oil
> 1 chicken (more than 2 lbs.), cut up as
>   for frying
> 1 small (8-oz.) can boiled onions, drained
> 1 No. 2 can tomatoes
> 1 can Italian tomato paste
> 2 No. 2 cans *garbanzos,* drained
> 2 green peppers, cut in thin strips and
>   seeds removed
> 1 teaspoon Worcestershire sauce
> Salt, pepper

Sauté the garlic in the olive oil, remove and add all the pieces of chicken (except the giblets—use them in another recipe), until they are a nice brown all over. Transfer to a deep casserole that has a lid. Add the onions, tomatoes, tomato paste, *garbanzos,* green peppers, Worcestershire sauce, salt and pepper to taste. Cover and bake in a 350° oven until the chicken is tender and the sauce is rich, thick and savory. Serves 4.

CHICKEN WITH CARAWAY SEEDS

Another simple but unusual way of cooking chicken.

> Olive oil
> 3 cloves garlic

    1 tablespoon caraway seeds
    1 teaspoon salt
    ½ teaspoon pepper
    1 roasting or frying chicken (3 to 3½ lbs.),
        cut up into serving pieces

In a skillet put olive oil about ¼ inch deep, the cloves of garlic, caraway seeds and salt and pepper. Marinate the chicken in this for about an hour. In the same oil brown the chicken slowly on all sides. Add a very small amount of water (¼ to ½ cup) and cook over a very low flame until tender, about 35 to 45 minutes. Serves 4.

CHICKEN WITH MUSHROOMS AND MARSALA

Simple but festive.

    1 medium-sized onion, chopped
    ¼ cup olive oil
    1 2½ to 3-lb. chicken, cut up as for frying
    ½ lb. mushrooms, sliced
    ¾ cup Marsala
        Salt, pepper

Brown the onion in the olive oil, and then add the cut-up chicken and brown it. Before it is entirely brown—say about a week-old tan at a good beach—add mushrooms, salt and pepper and ½ cup of the Marsala. Cover and cook slowly until the chicken is tender. This will be ½ hour to 40 minutes, depending on the age of the chicken and the kind of life it led before. Just before serving, add the other ¼ cup of Marsala. Serves 4.

CHILI CHICKEN

Almost no watching, simple, different and practically foolproof.

> 1 chicken (2½ to 3 lbs.), cut up
> 1 15-oz. can sweetened condensed milk
> Salt
> Black pepper
> 1½ teaspoons Worcestershire sauce
> 1½ teaspoons chili powder
> ½ teaspoon Tabasco sauce
> 1 teaspoon celery salt

Pour condensed milk into bowl and add remaining ingredients, except chicken. Stir well. Arrange chicken pieces, including liver and gizzard, skin side down in roasting pan large enough that pieces will be all in one layer. Pour mixture over chicken and bake in medium oven at 350° for 45 minutes. Then turn pieces over and continue baking for about 45 minutes or until done. Test for doneness by piercing drumstick or second joint with knife. If no pink meat shows at bone, it is done. If mixture becomes too dry, add water. No basting is required. Serve chicken pieces on warm platter and arrange around it baked potatoes split open, buttered and piled with green peas. Serves 4. This recipe works equally well for 2 chickens by increasing milk to 1½ cans and adding 1 teaspoon salt.

DILL CHICKEN

This is a sublimated interpretation of boiled chicken.

> 1 whole chicken (4 to 5 lbs.)
> 1 stalk celery, leaves and all
> 1 onion, quartered

  3 or 4 sprigs parsley
   Salt, pepper
  3 tablespoons fat, preferably butter
  3 tablespoons flour
  2 tablespoons finely chopped fresh dill
   (the dry just plain doesn't work)

Cover the whole chicken with water, add the celery, onion, parsley and seasoning; cover and simmer until the chicken is tender. Remove the chicken and keep warm. Make a thin cream sauce by melting the fat and blending with the flour, and add 2 cups of stock from the liquid the chicken was cooked in. Check for seasoning and add more if necessary. Stir in the freshly chopped dill and simmer for 2 or 3 minutes or until the flavors are well blended. Pour back over the whole boiled chicken and serve in a deep, warm platter or casserole. Serves 4 to 6.

NEW-FASHIONED OLD-FASHIONED
BOILED CHICKEN

This is a dish that sounds most improbable, but works beautifully and simply.

  1 fat old hen (5 to 7 lbs.)
   Salt, pepper
  4 strips bacon
   Aluminum foil

Salt and pepper the chicken inside and out. Lay it on a large piece of aluminum foil and put strips of bacon around the breast and under the wings. Wrap the chicken tightly in aluminum foil, pinching together so that there are no open places. Bake in a 350° oven for 3 hours without any fiddling or fussing; you will have a wonderful boiled chicken, no matter how incredible this seems. Serves 6 to 8.

POT-ROASTED FRYERS

2 whole fryers (1½ to 2 lbs. each)
  Salt, pepper
2 whole onions, peeled
4 strips bacon
2 tablespoons butter
⅓ cup red-wine vinegar, diluted with
  the same amount of water
1 tablespoon mixed pickling spice
2 cups cream
1 small bottle capers, drained
  Salt

Salt and pepper each chicken and dust lightly with flour. Put an onion in each one and wrap 2 strips of bacon around each bird. Melt the butter in the bottom of a Dutch oven and brown the chickens one at a time. Now fit both of them back into the Dutch oven carefully (you will need your largest size for this). Add the vinegar and water, pickling spice, cover and cook for about 1½ hours over a very low flame. Remove the chickens to a warm platter and keep it warm while making the gravy. Add the cream to the juices in the pan and cook until smooth and thick. This may be thickened by adding 1 tablespoon flour mixed with water to a thin paste, but the sauce will taste better when thickened by reducing. Strain and add the capers. Heat briefly before serving with the chicken. Serve with green salad and potatoes scalloped with pimientos. Serves 4.

POULET MARENGO

According to legend, this dish was first whipped up for Napoleon from ingredients on hand by an army cook just before the battle of Marengo, but like most legends, culinary or otherwise, has been modified as time goes on. This is traditionally garnished with fried eggs, which I prefer to omit, not liking fried eggs much.

> 1 2-lb. chicken, cut in 7 pieces
> 3 tablespoons olive oil
> 2 tablespoons butter
> 1 clove garlic, minced
> Salt, pepper
> ⅓ lb. mushrooms, sliced through caps and
> stems Japanese fashion
> 2 tablespoons Italian paste, thinned with
> 3 tablespoons chicken stock
> 1 jigger brandy
> ¼ cup dry white wine
> More chicken broth if necessary
> Croutons (stale cubes of bread, fried
> in olive oil)
> Parsley

Sauté the pieces of chicken in the mixture of olive oil and butter until brown on all sides. Turn the heat low, cover and cook for about 20 minutes or until the chicken is almost tender. Then add the mushrooms, the thinned tomato paste, brandy and dry white wine. Cook until tender, adding more chicken broth if the sauce becomes too short. Serve garnished with the fried croutons and parsley and, if you really want to, fried eggs. Serves 2 to 3.

PEG STERLING'S BLACK CHICKEN FRICASSEE

This fricassee ends up with a rich, black, natural gravy unsullied by any thickening, pleasing to those who object to the pallid appearance of the usual fricassee.

> 1 chicken (about 3 to 3½ lbs.), disjointed
> Salt, pepper
> Flour
> 3 tablespoons good fat, which is to say
>   chicken, bacon drippings or butter
> 1 onion, chopped fine
> 1 clove garlic, minced
> ¾ lb. mushrooms, sliced

Salt and pepper the chicken and roll in the flour. Brown the onion and garlic in the fat, add the chicken and cook until all are well browned. Add a cup of water and cook over a very low flame for about ¾ of an hour. Add more water if necessary to be slightly liquid but not sloshy. Add the mushrooms and cook for ¾ to 1 hour longer over a very low flame, adding a little more liquid if necessary. The sauce should be rich and black and fairly thick. Serves 4 to 6 if accompanied by a large bowl of fluffy rice, a good green salad and hot rolls (some of the partially baked kind).

PEG STERLING'S CHICKEN MANAGEMENT

This is one of the most practical ways of cooking chicken. All parts are used for several meals. You start out with a boiled chicken and lots of broth. Save the best parts, such as the breasts, for a fancy dish. Use the broth and some of the lesser parts, like legs and second joints (this, of course, is pure prejudice—I like the breasts), for such recipes as Mulligatawny. Put the giblets and wings in curried creole sauce or potpie.

> 1 chicken (5 to 7 lbs.)
> ½ lemon
>> Giblets, except the livers (cook briefly
>>> later before adding to the curried creole
>>> or potpie)
>> Celery tops
> 1 sliced onion
> 2 carrots, cut in pieces
>> Salt, pepper

Rub inside and out with the cut side of the lemon, cover with hot or boiling water, cook until the thickest pieces— say the second joints—are tender when pierced with a fork. Remove from the liquid, skim the fat off the top and strain, and use any two or three of the ways mentioned, or in any of the other recipes in the book that require cooked chicken.

OLD-FASHIONED OLD HEN STEW

Use an old hen for that true chickeny flavor.

        1 stewing chicken (4 to 5 lbs.), cut up
     3½ cups hot water
       ½ cup diced celery
       ½ cup diced carrot
        1 small onion, sliced
        2 teaspoons salt
        4 tablespoons cornstarch
        1 tablespoon diced pimiento

Wash chicken and pull excess fat from under the skin with your fingers. (Chicken fat can be rendered and used for cooking.) Place chicken, hot water, celery, carrot, onion and salt in Dutch oven. Cover and simmer 3 to 4 hours or until tender. Place chicken in hot serving dish. Combine cornstarch with ⅓ cup cold water. Gradually add to hot liquid and cook about 5 minutes or until thickened, stirring constantly. Add pimiento. Pour over chicken and serve immediately. Serves 6.

Use feet in the broth for extra flavor and richness. If you cook 2 or 3 pairs of chicken feet, the broth will taste better—be better for you, too.

SMOTHERED CHICKEN

Classic and beloved.

        2 chickens (2½ to 3 lbs.), cut up as for frying
          Flour, salt, pepper
       ⅓ cup shortening, preferably half butter
        2 cloves garlic, finely chopped
        8 to 10 small peeled potatoes
          More flour for thickening

Shake the chicken in a paper bag with the flour, salt and pepper until lightly coated. Add the garlic and chicken to the hot fat and brown evenly on all sides, a few pieces at a time. Drain on paper towels and keep warm until all is done; then return all the chicken to the pan with the potatoes. Add 1 cup water, cook over a very low flame until chicken and potatoes are tender, about 30 to 40 minutes. Remove chicken and potatoes to a hot platter and thicken the juices in the pan with 3 tablespoons flour mixed with enough cold water to make a thin paste. Cook until smooth and blended, adding more seasoning if necessary. Pour over the chicken on the platter. Serves 6 to 8.

EGG SAUCE FOR BOILED FOWL

This sauce, which adds so much to boiled fowl, is Southern or Italian and so on, depending on what cookbook you are reading at the time. The instructions are pretty similar, although sometimes the eggs are hard-cooked and sometimes used raw in the usual way as a thickening.

> 4 hard-cooked eggs
> 2 tablespoons butter
> 1 tablespoon flour
> 2 cups chicken broth
>   Salt, pepper (broth has some)
>   Capers, pleasant but unorthodox

Separate the egg yolks and the whites and mash the egg yolks, flour and butter together; stir in the hot stock slowly and let simmer for about 5 to 6 minutes. Take off the fire, season if necessary and add the finely chopped egg whites, and then if you wish add 3 tablespoons well-drained capers.

SMOTHERED CHICKEN WITH MUSHROOM AND PIMIENTO SAUCE

1 chicken (2½ to 3 lbs.), cut in two
6 strips breakfast bacon
⅛ lb. butter (¼ cup)
Salt, pepper

Salt and pepper chicken halves lightly and place skin side up in a large frying pan or in pan from broiler in range. Pour 1 cup water into pan and put butter into water. Place in oven, preheated to 450°, and cook uncovered about 15 minutes or until chicken is a nice even brown. Turn heat down to 350°, cover chicken with strips of bacon and cook until chicken is tender, about 45 minutes. Cut in smaller pieces, place on platter and pour sauce around pieces, not over them. For sauce:

½ lb. fresh mushrooms (or small can
    mushrooms)
⅛ lb. butter (¼ cup)
½ pint heavy cream (1 cup)
1 6½-oz. can pimientos, chopped
Salt, pepper
2 tablespoons flour

Sauté fresh mushrooms in the butter for 12 minutes. If canned mushrooms are used, no precooking is necessary. Add cream to fat and drippings in pan from which chicken was removed. Add pimiento and season to taste with salt and pepper. Boil 3 minutes; then add cooked mushrooms and thicken with flour which has been mixed with enough cold water to make a thin paste. Stir constantly while cooking slowly until sauce reaches a creamy thickness. Serves 4 to 5.

STEWED CHICKEN WITH DUMPLINGS

Basic and beloved.

>1 3½-lb. chicken, cut in pieces
>3 tablespoons fat from under the skin
>   of the chicken
>⅓ cup chopped onion
>   Salt, pepper

Melt the chicken fat and brown the pieces of seasoned chicken and the onion in it. Add 1 quart of hot water and cook in a pressure pan for 25 minutes at 15 lbs. pressure, being careful that the bulk does not fill more than ⅔ of the pan, or in a regular pan for about 2 hours. Reduce the pressure on the pan immediately and transfer the chicken to a deep platter and keep warm. Keep the pan liquid at simmering temperature ready for the dumplings that follow.

Dumplings:

>1 cup sifted flour
>2 teaspoons baking powder
>½ cup milk
>   Salt

Sift the dry ingredients into a bowl, add the milk and mix into a batter and drop from a spoon into the boiling juices in the pan. Cover and steam without pressure at a low heat for about 5 to 8 minutes. Add the dumplings to the chicken. Thicken the juice if desired with 1 tablespoon cornstarch mixed to a thin paste with water. Pour over the chicken dumplings. Serves 4 generously.

2

Broiled, Barbecued, Baked or Roasted

BROILED CHICKEN SAUTERNE

2 broilers (1½ lbs. each)
1 small onion, sliced
1 sprig parsley
1 cup sauterne
2 tablespoons lemon juice
Salt, pepper
2 tablespoons salad oil
1 tablespoon flour
1 tablespoon butter

Have the broilers split. Cut off necks, put in saucepan with the giblets, onion, parsley and 1 cup of cold water. Cover and simmer until giblets are tender. Add wine and strain. (This is the basting sauce during broiling.) Chop giblets fine and set aside. Sprinkle chicken with lemon juice, salt and pepper, and smooth with oil. Place skin side down in a shallow pan. Place low under broiler. Turn occasionally and baste frequently with wine sauce. When chickens are tender and well browned (this will take about 30 minutes) remove from pan. Thicken sauce with flour and butter blended together, add giblets, season to taste. Pour a little sauce over each serving. Serves 4.

GEORGIA'S BROILED CHICKEN BASTED WITH BUTTER, TARRAGON AND MUSTARD SAUCE

Simple and plain heavenly. While the recipe calls for a whole frying chicken, just the breasts—either fresh or frozen—may be used very deliciously.

> 1 chicken (about 2½ lbs.), cut in quarters,
>   or 2 lbs. breasts
> ¼ lb. (1 stick) butter
> 1 tablespoon tarragon vinegar
> 1 teaspoon dry English mustard
>   Salt, pepper
> ⅓ cup finely slivered toasted almonds

Drop the pieces into boiling water and let them stay without any heat for about 5 minutes. This is a Chinese trick that is very good—so often broiled chicken is not quite done. Drain and pat dry with a clean towel. Melt the butter, add the vinegar and mustard and blend well. Brush the quarters of chicken with this concoction and place skin side down in broiler about 7 to 9 inches from heat.

Broil slowly, turning occasionally and basting with some of the sauce, until the chicken is tender, nicely browned and crisp on the outside. It is done when the drumstick, pierced with a fork, shows no pink. Without the preliminary dip in boiling water, this will take about 50 minutes for this size chicken. With the hot quick dip, the time is cut from ⅓ to ½. Salt and pepper and serve with the rest of the sauce poured over the chicken and all of it sprinkled with the almonds. Serves 4 lightly. For ample appetites have 2 chickens and double the quantities for the sauce.

CHICKEN BLANKETED WITH PIMIENTOS AND ALMONDS

> 1 chicken (about 2½ lbs.), cut up as for frying
> Salt, pepper
> 1 6½-oz. can pimientos, finely chopped
> ⅓ cup finely chopped parsley
> ½ cup blanched, chopped almonds
> ⅓ to ½ cup softened, but not melted, butter

Salt and pepper the chicken and arrange in a shallow baking dish. Mix the pimientos, parsley, almonds and butter into a sort of paste. Spread over the pieces of chicken and bake in a 325° oven for about 50 minutes or until the chicken is tender when pierced in the thigh with a fork and no pink shows. Serves 4.

CHICKEN BREASTS MARINATED IN WHITE WINE WITH JUNIPER BERRIES

This is very close to soaking your chicken in your Martini; in fact, the recipe may be made using vermouth instead of the white wine.

> 8 chicken breasts
> ⅔ cup dry white wine
> 1 or 2 tablespoons juniper berries
> ½ teaspoon rosemary
> 3 tablespoons butter
> Salt, pepper

Arrange the chicken breasts in a shallow baking dish, pour the wine over them and add the juniper berries and rosemary. Let stand for at least several hours. Bake in the same dish in the marinade in a 350° oven for about 50 minutes, adding the butter, salt and pepper, and basting from time to time with an oversized eye dropper that is called a baster. Serve in the same dish in the basting sauce and accompany with tiny new potatoes boiled in their skins, green beans with butter, a dash of nutmeg and tomato aspic salad. Serves 4.

CHICKEN BREASTS WITH WHITE WINE AND WHITE GRAPES

Another dish that proves some of the simplest cooking is the best.

8 chicken breasts
4 tablespoons butter
Salt and pepper
½ cup dry white wine
¾ cup white seedless grapes

Oven-roast the chicken breasts spread with butter in a 350° oven and add the wine after ½ hour's time, basting occasionally with the wine and butter in the pan for about 50 minutes or until tender.

Just before the breasts are done add the white grapes that have been peeled—when you feel like doing a very fancy act—otherwise just leave their skins on. Serves 4 with a menu such as fresh peas and spoon bread and a salad of Belgian endive.

CHICKEN ROASTED IN CHAMPAGNE

> 1 roasting chicken (3 to 3½ lbs.)
> 2 tablespoons butter
>   Salt, pepper
> 1 cup champagne, preferably dry (a split
>   will do though it is a few tablespoons
>   less than 1 cup)
> 3 egg yolks
> 2 cups heavy cream
> 1 truffle, sliced (if you are being this lavish)

Prepare the chicken for roasting, trussing in the usual way and rubbing generously with the butter and sprinkling with salt and pepper. Roast according to basic directions, basting with the champagne and the juices that mingle with it in the pan, for an hour or more in a 350° oven. When done remove the chicken from the juices and keep warm while you stir the juices in the pan into the egg yolks that have been beaten with the heavy cream. Heat in the top of a double boiler and pour over the chicken before serving. Arrange the truffle, sliced thin, over the chicken and serve. Serves 4.

CHICKEN ROASTED ON A ROTISSERIE

After this many recipes I shouldn't be prejudiced, but this really is one of the simplest ways of cooking chicken and one of the very best, and it's also a fine act to put on for your guests. The meat is tender and moist and the skin wonderfully crunchy, and it's all done with no effort. Also you don't need dogs to turn the spit as in medieval days; the local power company does that job. This was done on a Rotiss-o-mat, but the basic principles are approximately the same for all brands, and the instructions vary only slightly.

> 1 chicken (about 5 to 6 lbs.)
> Salt, pepper
> Worcestershire sauce
> Butter

Have the butcher truss the chicken or do it yourself according to basic instructions. This must be done or it will drag a wing or so, ballocksing up the machine. Rub the chicken with salt, pepper, Worcestershire sauce and slightly softened butter. Stick the skewer through the chicken lengthwise, being careful to get it fairly in the middle so that the weight is balanced. Put the holding pins on each end to secure it. Place in position, turn on the heat to medium and let go for about 1½ hours. That's all. Serves about 4. While this size chicken usually will serve more it tastes so good this way that everyone eats extra.

CHICKEN SMOTHERED IN ONION RINGS

> 1 lb. fresh or frozen chicken breasts
> 1 large onion, sliced very thin
> 3 tablespoons butter
> 1 tablespoon lemon juice
> Salt and pepper
> 1 teaspoon Worcestershire sauce

Arrange the chicken breasts (thawed, if frozen) in a shallow buttered casserole. Blanket with the onion rings. Dot with butter; then sprinkle with lemon juice, salt, pepper and Worcestershire sauce. Bake in 350° oven until tender and done, about 1 hour. Serves 4.

CHICKEN THIGHS OR BREASTS BASTED WITH BUTTER AND VERMOUTH

This dish seems almost too simple to be as good as it is.

>2 lbs. chicken breasts or thighs
>¼ cup butter
>¼ cup dry French vermouth
>Salt, pepper

Arrange in a shallow pottery baking dish and dot with the butter. Pour in the vermouth, sprinkle with salt and pepper and bake in a 350° oven 45 to 55 minutes. Baste occasionally with the juices in the pan. Serve in the juices. Serves 4.

CHINESE CHICKEN, AMERICAN ROTISSERIE STYLE

This may be done by soaking pieces of chicken and then roasting in a 350° oven for 50 minutes, but a whole chicken spitted on a rotisserie is something extra special.

>⅓ cup soya sauce
>2 tablespoons salad oil
>1 teaspoon dry mustard
>½ teaspoon powdered ginger
>1 clove garlic, minced
>Pepper (the soya sauce is salty)
>1 3½-lb. roasting chicken

Mix all the ingredients together except the chicken, and brush the chicken frequently with the mixture over a period of 1 hour so that it soaks in well. Affix to the spit in rotisserie according to its directions. Turn to medium heat and let twirl for about 1½ hours. Serves 4 or 5.

CRISP BAKED CHICKEN

For those who like their chicken crisp and crunchy but
not fried.

>   1 2½ to 3-lb. chicken, cut up for frying
>   3 tablespoons salad oil
>   2 teaspoons salt
>   ¼ teaspoon pepper
>   3 cups corn flakes

Rub chicken with one of the tablespoons of salad oil, salt
and pepper. Crush corn flakes into fine crumbs. Roll
chicken in crumbs until well coated. Put chicken in
greased shallow baking pan and sprinkle with remaining
oil. Bake in very hot oven (500°) 10 to 15 minutes or until
browned; turn heat down to 325° and bake chicken 30
minutes longer or until it is tender. Serve it at once.
Serves 4.

DEVILED CHICKEN THIGHS OR LEGS

>   2 lbs. chicken thighs (second joints) or legs
>   3 tablespoons butter
>   Salt, pepper
>   2 teaspoons dry English mustard
>   ½ cup cream or milk

Sauté the chicken thighs or legs in the butter, adding salt
until well browned. Arrange side by side in a shallow
baking dish and pour the drippings from the pan over
them. Mix the mustard into a thin paste by adding ½ cup
water slowly. Mix with the milk and pour over the
chicken. Bake in a 350° oven 30 to 40 minutes or until
the chicken is tender. Serves 4.

GOLDEN CHICKEN

A basic procedure for roasting a plump young chicken slowly and lovingly. For an unusual flavor, instead of stuffing put a juicy apple inside, tie the legs to the tail and roast away. A chicken that weighs 2½ to 3½ lbs., ready to cook, will require about 1½ to 2 hours at 350°.

Stuffing and Trussing:

Stuff chicken just before roasting—not ahead of time. Stuffing prepared in advance must be refrigerated. Allow 1¼ cups stuffing per pound ready to cook or 1 cup dressed weight.

1. Rub cavity of bird with ½ to 1 teaspoon salt.
2. Stuff body and wishbone cavities *lightly.*
3. Close by placing skewers across the body opening and lace shut with cord.
4. Tie drumsticks together; then tie securely to tail.
5. Fasten neck skin to back with skewer. Shape wings "akimbo" style; bring tips onto back.
6. Brush skin with melted fat. Poultry seasoning may be sprinkled over the surface.

Roasting:

1. Place trussed bird breast down on a rack at least ½ inch high in a shallow open pan.
2. Cover top of chicken with fat-moistened thin cloth. Do not wrap bird in the cloth.
3. Roast at moderate temperature (350°). Allow 25 to 30 minutes per pound. Meat thermometer thrust into meaty part of leg and not touching bone should register 185° when done.
4. DO NOT SEAR. DO NOT ADD WATER. DO NOT COVER.

5. If cloth dries during cooking, moisten cloth with fat from bottom of pan.

6. Turn bird breast up when about ¾ done. Roast until tender.

7. Test for doneness: Move leg by grasping end of the bone. The drumstick-thigh joint breaks or moves easily. Or, drumstick meat is very soft when pressed between fingers. Do not pierce meat with fork.

SIMPLE AND SAVORY BARBECUED CHICKEN

1 chicken (2½ to 3½-lb. boiler-fryer),
    cut up as for frying
2 tablespoons fat
1 medium-sized onion, chopped
1 8-oz. can tomato sauce
½ tablespoon prepared mustard
1 teaspoon salt
1 tablespoon vinegar
2 tablespoons brown sugar
1 tablespoon Worcestershire sauce

Brown chicken pieces for 15 to 20 minutes in frying pan containing the fat, turning occasionally. Remove chicken to roasting pan. Cook onions in frying pan until golden in color. Add rest of ingredients and ½ cup water. Simmer 10 minutes while stirring well, and pour over chicken. Bake in a moderate oven (350°) for an hour, basting frequently. If sauce becomes too dry, add a little water. For extra crispness increase heat to 500° or place under broiler for last few minutes. Serves 4 to 5.

SVEND'S ROAST CHICKEN STUFFED
WITH PARSLEY

This dish in its Danish perfection is made with several baby chickens, seldom seen here. They are about the size of a squab and look much too young to be away from their mother.

> 1 ready-to-cook young chicken (2 to 3 lbs.)
> Salt
> 1 bunch parsley
> 1 cup melted butter
> ½ cup heavy cream
> 2 cups broth or water
> 3 tablespoons flour
> 1 slice onion
> 1 stalk celery, sliced
> 1 teaspoon celery seed

Salt the chicken generously inside and outside. Cut the stems off the parsley and chop; then mix with the butter. Put in the cavity of the chicken. (This is my version. Svend just puts the whole bunch of parsley inside.) Butter skin thoroughly and place chicken on rack in a shallow pan. Roast at moderate temperature (350°) until tender, 1½ to 2 hours. Baste occasionally during the roasting with melted butter and juices from the bottom of the pan. About ½ hour before done pour ½ cup cream over the chicken. (This is authentically Danish and very good, though Svend's version doesn't include cream.) Place chicken on warm serving platter while preparing the gravy. For 2 cups of gravy use 3 tablespoons of the pan drippings, 3 tablespoons flour and 2 cups of chicken broth made by cooking the giblets and the neck in water with onion, celery or celery salt. Makes 4 servings.

ORIOLE'S BAKED CHICKEN

This turns out real crispy and is a favorite with people who don't like the usual fried chicken or shouldn't eat it for various reasons. Oriole (a very pretty girl, not a bird) says that the original version was garnished with 6 slices of bacon and parsley, but she never uses the bacon.

> 1 3-lb. chicken, cut up as for frying
> 1 egg
> 2 teaspoons salt
>   Bread crumbs
> 2 tablespoons butter
>   Chopped parsley

Break the egg into a bowl with the salt and beat. Drop the chicken in the bowl and stir around until all is well covered. Then roll each piece in bread crumbs, put in a well-buttered casserole and dot with butter. Cover and bake in a 425° oven for 1¼ hours. Sprinkle with finely chopped parsley. Serves 4.

OVEN-BARBECUED CHICKEN

Ideally all barbecuing should be done outdoors with the good smell of smoke hovering around, but this is good in the oven too.

    2 chickens (2½ to 3½ lbs.), cut in half—
        necks, gizzards, hearts
    1 large onion
    1 clove garlic
    1 teaspoon sugar
    2 teaspoons dry mustard
        Salt, pepper
    ½ teaspoon garlic salt
    ¼ teaspoon cayenne
    4 tablespoons Worcestershire sauce
    1½ cups tomato juice
    ¾ cup vinegar
        Chicken livers
    ½ lb. mushrooms (pleasant but not obligatory)

Lay chicken skin side down in a shallow open pan. Add sliced onion, gizzards, hearts and garlic. Pour in water to fill pan about ¾ inch. Cook in moderately hot oven (375°) 1 hour, turning occasionally, until there is only half as much water.

Meanwhile, prepare barbecue sauce: Mix sugar, mustard, salt, pepper, garlic salt and cayenne in saucepan. Add Worcestershire sauce, tomato juice, vinegar and ¾ cup water. Heat to boiling and pour all sauce over chicken. Baste chicken with hot sauce about every 10 minutes, leaving a pool of sauce in rib cage when halves are turned ribs up.

Cook until chicken is tender and sauce is reduced to a rich gravy, about 1½ to 2 hours longer. For larger chick-

uld sauce thicken before chicken is
p boiling water. Drop sliced mush-
to sauce about 15 minutes before
 chicken to hot platter and serve the
eld: 4 halves or 8 quarters, or 4 to 8

ss place well-basted chicken skin side
Vatch it—3 minutes may be ample!
icken on outdoor grill use same sauce,
olying frequently with spoon or stick

ICKEN WITH A LEMON AND
R BARBECUE SAUCE

ened to men who are one-dish cookers
th with horrible preciosity about the
 they need to make *their* barbecue
o tasting just as fiery as all the others,
implicity of this one based on a recipe
sco people. This is my interpretation.

ted butter
h lemon juice, freshly squeezed
n Tabasco sauce (more or less
   according to individual tastes)
1 teaspoon salt
1 roasting chicken (3½ to 5 lbs.)

With a pastry brush or other soft brush, brush the chicken generously with the sauce. Put on the skewer in the Rotiss-o-mat or whatever your rotisserie is called. Turn the indicator to medium heat and let whirl around for 1½ hours. Swab occasionally with the sauce. Serves 4.

CHICKEN-ALMOND CASSEROLE

1 8-ounce package noodles.
2 tblsps. butter
2 tblsps. minced onion
1 cup thin-sliced celery
2 tblsps. flour
¾ tsp. dry mustard
2½ tsps. salt
⅛ tsp. pepper
2½ cups milk
2 tsps. Worcestershire sauce
1 cup grated or shredded American cheese
2 cups diced cooked chicken or turkey
¼ cup chopped pimiento
¼ cup chopped green pepper
1 cup roasted almonds,
1½ cup buttered soft bread crumbs

Cook noodles according package directions until alm... tender; drain and rinse w cold water. Melt butter in saucepan, add onion and cele... and cook and stir until tran... parent, about five minute... Blend in flour, mustard, s... and pepper. Add milk and W... cestershire. Cook until sauce smooth and thickened. Stir cheese, chicken, pimiento, gre... pepper, well-drained nood... and half of the almonds. Tu... into a shallow baking dish ar sprinkle with crumbs. Bake in maining almonds. Bake in 400-degree oven about 20 mi... utes, or until thoroughly heate... and lightly browned on to... Makes eight to 10 servings.

ROAST CHICKEN BREASTS WITH SLICED LEMON

This combination of flavors is so simple, so natural and so good it seems strange that it is usually found only in books on foreign food. It is appealing to the current inclination for delicate and uncluttered food.

> 4 fresh chicken breasts—or 1 package
>   frozen ones, thawed
> ½ stick butter (¼ cup)
> 1 large lemon (preferably the thin-skinned
>   type), sliced thin
> Salt, pepper

Arrange the chicken breasts skin side up in a shallow buttered casserole, pretty enough to come to the table. Sprinkle generously with salt and pepper, and dot the breasts with butter; then arrange the thin slices of lemon so that all the pieces of chicken are covered with the lemon. The circles will overlap, of course. Roast uncovered in a 350° oven for about 50 minutes—give or take a few minutes— until the chicken is tender. From time to time add the rest of the butter and baste with the juices in the pan. This is good cold, and fine for a picnic if the lemon slices are removed before packing each breast decoratively and tidily in aluminum foil. Serves 4.

ROAST CHICKEN WITH ANCHOVY BUTTER

This is somewhat Russian.

> 1 roasting chicken (3½ to 5½ lbs.)
> 6 anchovies, mashed
> ¼ cup sweet butter

Mix the anchovies with the sweet butter until a well-blended odorous mess. Spread evenly all over the chicken and roast the usual way. Serves 4 to 6.

VERY SPECIAL BROILED CHICKEN

Broiled slowly and evenly these birds acquire a delectable golden color with a wonderful flavor unlike any other. It's the lemon and sugar that does it, strange as it may sound.

>   2 plump broiler-fryers (2 to 3 lbs.)
>   1 lemon
>   4 teaspoons salt
>   ½ teaspoon black pepper
>   1 teaspoon paprika
>   ½ cup melted butter
>   2 tablespoons sugar

Place chickens, cut in half, in broiling pan. Rub entire surface of each half chicken with cut lemon, squeezing so that there is plenty of juice. Sprinkle with mixture of salt, pepper and paprika. Coat each half thoroughly with melted butter, using brush or cloth. Then sprinkle lightly with sugar.

Leave in broiler pan (not rack) with skin side down. Place pan in broiler 5 to 7 inches from heat. Chicken should be broiled slowly. Regulate heat or pan position so that chicken just begins to brown lightly in 10 minutes. Turn and brush with fat 2 or 3 times during broiling to brown and cook evenly. Total cooking time varies from 35 to 50 minutes. The chicken is done when meat on the thickest part of the drumstick cuts easily and there is no pink color visible.

Serve on large, warm platter; garnish with broiled tomato halves and parsley. Serves 4 to 8.

ROAST CHICKEN WITH UNDERSKIN DRESSING

1 roasting chicken (3½ to 5 lbs.)
2 cans Sell's liver *pâté*
1 jigger cognac
  Salt
3 good-sized onions, finely chopped
1 bunch parsley, finely chopped
½ cup butter

Mix the *pâté* with the cognac. Loosen the skin of the chicken by running your hand between the skin and the flesh. Pat the mixture under the skin into nice symmetrical curves so your chicken will have good plump contours in the best American fashion. Let stand with the underskin dressing in the refrigerator for several hours. About 1 hour before roasting remove from the refrigerator and let come to room temperature. Just before roasting mix the onion, parsley and butter together, having salted the chicken well inside and out. Fill it with the parsley and onion mixture, and roast according to basic directions. Serves 4 to 6.

TARRAGON CHICKEN

This is the simple and I think perfect recipe, though you can get pretty complicated in some versions of this dish.

> 8 chicken breasts, fresh or frozen
> 24 sprigs of tarragon (fresh or the kind
>   that comes in jars of vinegar)
> 1 stick butter (¼ lb.)
>   Salt, pepper

Arrange the chicken breasts in a shallow baking dish. Butter the skin and arrange 3 sprigs of tarragon on each breast. Salt and pepper. Divide the rest of the butter into 8 pieces and put 1 piece on each breast. Put in a 325° oven and roast for about 50 minutes, basting occasionally with one of those oversized eye droppers, using the butter in the pan. Serves 4.

3

Casseroles and Potpies

BAKED CHICKEN IN WINE SAUCE

1 3-lb. broiler-fryer chicken,
    cut in frying pieces
¾ cup flour
1½ teaspoons salt
¼ teaspoon pepper
⅛ lb. butter
½ cup chicken stock
½ cup sauterne wine

Mix flour, salt and pepper and roll chicken pieces in it.
Sauté chicken in butter until golden brown. Place pieces
in a baking dish with chicken stock made from neck and
giblets cooked in 2 to 3 cups water and wine. Cover dish
and bake in slow oven at 325° for about 1 hour, or until
largest pieces are tender. Serve with broccoli or garnish
with parsley. Serves 4.

CASSEROLE OF CHICKEN

1 young chicken (2½ to 3 lbs.)
¼ cup flour
  Salt, pepper
1 teaspoon paprika
½ cup fat for frying
⅛ teaspoon or pinch each nutmeg and mace
  Grated rind of a lemon
¼ cup broth
2 strips bacon
  Fried stuffing balls (pleasant but
    not necessary)

Disjoint and cut chicken into serving pieces. Include giblets and neck. Coat with flour blended with seasonings. Brown well in the fat. Place in casserole, adding nutmeg, mace, lemon rind and the broth. Place strips of bacon on top. Cover. Bake in a moderate oven (350°) until tender when pricked with a fork, about 40 to 50 minutes. Meanwhile, make the stuffing balls:

2 cups sieved bread crumbs
1 tablespoon melted butter
1 tablespoon chopped parsley
1 teaspoon thyme
½ teaspoon grated lemon rind
1 egg yolk
¼ cup milk
  Salt and pepper

Blend ingredients, adding salt and pepper to taste. Roll into 20 1-inch balls. Fry to a golden brown in fat used for browning chicken. Place on top of chicken 20 minutes before the chicken is tender. Serves 4.

BAKED CHICKEN SALAD

This is a silly-sounding dish that works out surprisingly well. Good for a large group because it can be prepared beforehand and baked briefly just before serving.

3 cups cooked or canned chicken, cut in
    large dice
1 cup blanched, slivered almonds
1 4-oz. can pimientos, cut in strips
1½ cups mayonnaise
¼ cup lemon juice
1 medium-sized onion, chopped fine
2 cups diced parboiled celery
Salt, paprika
1 cup potato chips or corn flakes, crumbled
½ cup sharp Cheddar or Parmesan cheese,
    grated

Mix all the ingredients together, thinning the mayonnaise with the lemon juice, except the potato chips or corn flakes and cheese, and turn into a shallow buttered casserole. Cover the top with potato chips and sprinkle them with the cheese. Bake in 350° oven 20 to 25 minutes, although a few minutes longer will not hurt. Serves 6 to 8.

BETTY'S CHICKEN TETRAZZINI

½ package noodles
2 cups diced cooked chicken
1 10½-oz. can condensed cream-of-mushroom
    soup
½ cup milk
⅓ cup finely freshly grated Parmesan (don't
    be streamlined and use the already grated—
    it's no better than sawdust)

Cook the noodles in boiling salted water until almost done but not quite, drain and put in a casserole. Pour in the chicken which has been mixed with the mushroom soup and milk. Sprinkle with the cheese and bake in a 350° oven 15 to 20 minutes. Serves 4.

BONED CHICKEN WITH MUSHROOMS

Another delicate and delicious interpretation of boiled chicken. This time an Italian version.

>   2 2½-lb. chickens, cut up as for frying
>   5 or 6 stalks of celery, cut up
>   1 medium-sized onion, diced
>   3 tablespoons flour
>   1 cup Marsala or muscatel
>   Salt, pepper
>   1½ lbs. mushrooms (chop stems fine
>   but leave caps whole)
>   3 tablespoons olive oil
>   1 clove garlic
>   Buttered bread crumbs
>   ⅓ cup chopped almonds

Boil the chickens and the giblets with the celery and onion in 3 to 4 cups water about 50 minutes or until tender. Remove the pieces of chicken and giblets and thicken the stock by mixing the flour with enough cold water to make a thin paste and adding to the stock. Cook briefly and add the Marsala or muscatel and seasoning. Remove the meat from the bones. Sauté the mushrooms in the olive oil with the garlic. Remove the garlic. Put the boned chicken, mushrooms and sauce in a casserole in layers, cover with the buttered bread crumbs and sprinkle with the chopped almonds. Brown and serve. Serves 6 generously.

CASSEROLE OF CHICKEN WITH SWEETBREADS

Bland and delicate.

>1 pair sweetbreads
>2 cups diced boiled chicken, preferably the white meat
>1 pint cream
>1 tablespoon cornstarch
>Milk
>2 egg yolks, slightly beaten
>1 tablespoon butter
>Salt, pepper
>¼ cup sherry

Poach the sweetbreads in boiling water with 1 tablespoon vinegar or lemon juice and 1 teaspoon salt over a very low flame for 20 minutes. Remove and plunge into cold water. Pull off the membrane and cut the sweetbreads into ½-inch cubes about the same size as the pieces of chicken. Cook the cream in the top of a double boiler, thickening with cornstarch mixed to a thin paste with a little milk. Add the beaten egg yolk and blend. Stir in the butter, salt, pepper and sherry. When slightly thickened add the chicken and sweetbreads. Serve on toast. Serves 4.

CHICKEN AND CRANBERRIES IN ONION BISCUIT ROLL

An off-the-kitchen-shelves dish that tastes as if you had spent hours doing it.

>Drop biscuit dough made from a good ready-mix

2 medium-sized onions, chopped fine, or
   1 extra large one
2 cups diced, cooked or canned chicken
1 1-lb. can whole-cranberry sauce
1 teaspoon dried mint
   Salt, pepper

Mix the onion with the biscuit dough and pat out (don't roll—it must be thick) onto a cookie sheet in a rectangle about 6 by 12 inches. Break up the cranberry sauce with a fork and mix gently with the chicken. Spoon the mixture down the middle of the biscuit dough, and then sprinkle with the mint, salt and pepper. Bring the sides together, pinch together carefully, and then pinch the ends together. Bake in a 400° oven 20 to 25 minutes, or until the biscuit is brown and done. Transfer carefully to a small warm platter and serve by cutting in thin slices as you would French bread. Serves 4.

CHICKEN BREASTS BAKED WITH CREAM AND CHEESE

1 lb. fresh or frozen chicken breasts
1 large Bermuda onion, cut in thick slices
1½ cups heavy cream
⅓ cup grated Parmesan cheese
   Salt, pepper

Arrange the breasts—or legs or second joints, if you prefer—in a casserole with a thick slice of onion over each piece. Salt and pepper. Pour the cream over and sprinkle the top with the grated cheese. Bake in a 350° oven about 45 minutes to 1 hour or until a rich thick savory mess. Serves 4.

CHICKEN AND GREEN NOODLES WITH SHERRY SAUCE

1 chicken (2½ to 3 lbs.), cut up as for frying
Salt
½ lb. flat green spinach noodles
2 tablespoons butter
⅓ cup butter (6 tablespoons)
⅓ cup flour
Salt, paprika
¼ lb. fresh mushrooms sliced thin, or canned
sliced mushrooms (which will not be as
good)
⅓ cup sherry
¼ cup grated Parmesan cheese (when you
grate your own it is much better than
that desiccated stuff you get in envelopes)

Put the pieces of chicken, without the giblets, in a pressure pan with 3 cups of water and the salt. Cover and
bring up to pressure and cook for 20 minutes at 10 lbs.
pressure. Reduce pressure immediately, and when chick-
en is cool enough to handle remove skin and bones and cut
in good mouth-size pieces. Naturally this may be cooked
in any heavy-bottomed pan, allowing a longer time and
doubling the liquid. The time will vary according to the
tenderness of the chicken, but allow at least 1 hour. Save
the liquid. Cook the noodles in a large amount of boiling
salted water until just barely tender. Drain; rinse with
very hot water. Drain again. Put in the bottom of a casserole and add the 2 tablespoons of butter.

Strew the pieces of chicken over the noodles and pour

the sauce made this way over all: melt the next ⅓ cup butter, add the flour and cook slowly, blending well, until the floury taste is gone. Add the liquid from the pressure cooker and, stirring constantly all the while, cook until there is a smooth creamy sauce. Add salt, paprika, mushrooms and sherry. Pour this sauce over the chicken and noodles and sprinkle the top with the grated cheese. Bake in a 400° oven until the top is brown and bubbling which will be 20 to 25 minutes. Serves 4.

CHICKEN AND GREEN VEGETABLE CASSEROLE

1 chicken (about 3 to 3½ lbs.), cut up
⅓ cup butter
2 bunches spring onions, tops and
    bottoms, chopped
2 zuccini, sliced thick but not peeled
½ lb. green beans or 1 package frozen
    green beans
1 lb. small tender okra or 1 No. 2½ can
1 eggplant, peeled and diced
2 green peppers, chopped and seeds removed
2 cups chicken broth
1 lemon, sliced thin
    Salt, pepper

Sauté the chicken in the butter until brown on all sides. Add the onions and cook them until slightly browned. Put all in a casserole with the drippings from the skillet and all the other vegetables. Cook until the chicken and vegetables are tender. Serves 4 to 6.

CHICKEN AND MUSHROOM CASSEROLE

1 cup stale, coarsely crumbled bread crumbs
 mixed with ¼ cup (4 tablespoons)
 melted butter
2 cups sliced or coarsely diced cooked or
 canned chicken
¼ lb. mushrooms, sliced through the caps
 and the stems
½ cup heavy cream
¾ cup chicken bouillon
¼ cup white wine
 Salt, pepper, paprika

Put half the buttered bread crumbs on the bottom of a casserole, arrange the chicken on top and strew the sliced mushrooms over that. Mix the cream, chicken broth and white wine with salt, pepper and paprika, and pour over the chicken and mushrooms. Sprinkle the top with the rest of the bread crumbs and bake in a 350° oven for 20 minutes or until the crumbs are browned and bubbling. Serves 4.

CHICKEN AND NEW POTATO HASH WITH MUSHROOMS AND SOUR CREAM

A straight-from-the-pantry-shelf dish with personality.

1 No. 2 can tiny new potatoes, drained
3 tablespoons bacon drippings (this is
 important—if you don't have the
 bacon drippings, cook bacon and
 get some)
1 can (6 ozs.) boned chicken or 12 ozs.
 diced—depending upon how lavish you feel

¼ cup fresh mushrooms, sliced
1 tablespoon butter
1 cup sour cream
Salt, pepper

Brown the new potatoes in the bacon fat, add the boned or diced chicken and swish around until brown and well flavored with the bacon. Add the mushrooms, sautéed in the butter, the sour cream, salt and pepper. Warm the sour cream but do not let it boil. If it does it will taste all right but it won't look so pretty. Serves 2.

CHICKEN AND STUFFED GREEN OLIVE CASSEROLE

2 lbs. chicken thighs
1 4 or 5-oz. jar green olives, stuffed with
pimientos, drained and sliced
3 tablespoons butter
3 tablespoons flour
2 cups chicken broth
1 cup milk
Salt, pepper
3 or 4 medium-sized potatoes, peeled
and sliced thin

In a deep buttered casserole arrange 1 layer of chicken thighs and 1 thin layer of sliced stuffed olives. Then add sauce made by melting the butter, blending the flour, adding the chicken broth and then the milk slowly, stirring until smooth and thickened. Season with salt and pepper. Add a layer of the sliced potatoes and repeat until all the ingredients are used. Bake in a 350° oven about 1 hour or until the meat is tender and the top brown and bubbling. Serves 4.

CHICKEN AND ONION PUDDING, YORKSHIRE FASHION

1 chicken (2½ lbs.), cut up as for frying
Salt, pepper
3 tablespoons butter
1 No. 2 can small boiled onions, drained
½ cup melted butter, chicken fat or
    bacon drippings
2 eggs
1 cup milk
1 cup sifted flour
1 teaspoon baking flour
½ teaspoon salt

Salt and pepper the chicken and sauté in the butter until golden brown. Cover and cook over a very low flame until the chicken is tender. Place in a casserole with the onions and put in the oven, preheated to 350°, to get hot while you make the batter. Beat the eggs. Add the drippings, milk and the dry ingredients which have been sifted together. Beat until it isn't lumpy—this should be a very thin batter. Take the casserole out of the oven and pour the batter over the hot chicken and onions. Bake in a 350° oven for about 30 minutes. Giblet gravy is good with this. (See page 112.) Serves 4.

CHICKEN AND PORK CASSEROLE

More or less Philippine fashion.

1 2 to 2½-lb. chicken, cut up as for frying
1 lb. pork, preferably with considerable fat,
    cut into 1-inch cubes
2 tablespoons bacon drippings or lard
½ cup vinegar

4 cloves garlic
2 tablespoons soy sauce
Salt, pepper
1 tablespoon flour
1 chicken liver, cooked and mashed
Hot cooked rice

Sauté the chicken and pour in a skillet with the lard, browning on all sides. Add the vinegar, garlic, soy sauce, salt and pepper. Cover and simmer about 1 hour or until the meat is tender and the pork has had ample time to become well cooked. Transfer the meat to a warm platter in a warm place and strain the liquid. If you wish, thicken the liquid slightly with flour mixed to a thin paste with water. Add salt and pepper to taste and the liver; pour over the meat and serve with hot rice. Serves 4 to 6.

CHICKEN-BROCCOLI CASSEROLE

A simplified version of the dish called Chicken Divan served in most French-American restaurants.

1 package frozen broccoli
1 cup diced cooked or canned chicken
1 10½-oz. can cream-of-chicken soup
2 tablespoons California sherry wine
Buttered fine bread crumbs and/or
  grated Parmesan cheese

Cook the broccoli according to directions on wrapper. Drain well and arrange in the bottom of a greased casserole. Top with the diced cooked chicken. Blend the chicken soup and sherry wine together gently to make a sauce, and pour over the broccoli and chicken. Sprinkle with bread crumbs and/or grated cheese. Bake in a 400° oven for about 15 minutes or until bubbly. Serves 3 or 4.

CHICKEN BAKED IN CREAM WITH SPRING ONIONS

Simple, succulent and savory.

> 1 chicken (about 2½ lbs.), cut up as for frying
> ¼ cup butter
> 8 spring onions or scallions, tops and
>   bottoms, chopped
> Salt, pepper
> 1 teaspoon Worcestershire sauce
> 1 pint cream, light or heavy, depending on
>   your waistline

Sauté the pieces of chicken in the butter until a light golden brown. Transfer to a casserole with a lid. Sprinkle with the chopped onions, both the green and white part. Pour over this the fat and juices from the pan. Salt and pepper the chicken and onions. Mix the Worcestershire sauce with the cream and pour over the chicken. Cover tightly and bake in a 350° oven for about 1 hour or until the chicken is tender and the cream cooked down to a lovely, clotted sauce (and it is supposed to look that way). Serves 4.

CHICKEN BAKED IN SOUR CREAM

As this bakes, the sour cream will thicken and clot into a simple and delectable sauce that tenderizes while it cooks.

> 1 chicken (2½ lbs.), cut up as for frying
> ¼ teaspoon each powdered ginger,
>   dry mustard and powdered marjoram
> ⅓ cup olive oil
> Salt, pepper

1 pint sour cream
3 tablespoons lemon juice
1 tablespoon grated lemon peel

Pick the chicken over, if necessary. Mix the ginger, mustard and marjoram together and dust each piece of chicken, except the giblets, with these spices. Heat the oil in a skillet and sauté the chicken until a nice golden brown. Remove from the pan, drain briefly on paper towels and spread out in a shallow casserole so there will be just 1 layer of the meat. Salt and pepper generously. Mix the sour cream with the lemon juice and spread over the chicken. Sprinkle the top with the grated lemon peel. Bake in a 300° oven until the chicken is tender when pierced with a fork, or about 1 hour. Serves 4.

CHICKEN LEGS BAKED IN SOUR CREAM

1 lb. fresh or frozen chicken legs
    or drumsticks (about 8)
2 tablespoons butter
1 large onion, sliced thin, or
    2 medium-sized ones
Salt, pepper
1 cup (½ pt.) sour cream
Paprika
¼ cup finely chopped fresh parsley

Brown the chicken legs in butter. Arrange a bed of the onion rings in the bottom of a shallow casserole and the chicken legs on top of that. Sprinkle with salt and pepper and spread the sour cream over the top. Sprinkle with paprika and sprinkle parsley on top. Bake in a 350° oven until the legs are tender when pricked with a fork and no pink shows. Serves 4.

CHICKEN CASSEROLE WITH CAPERS AND OLIVES

This dish varies in national origin, depending on who gave it to you. The person who gave this to me said it was Italian, but I've seen a Honduran version, a Mexican version, and it seems to me even more versions that I don't remember right now.

1 chicken (5 to 6 lbs.), cut in pieces
4 tablespoons olive oil
2 cloves garlic, cut in half
1 No. 2½ can tomatoes
1 can Italian tomato paste
1 large onion, chopped
2 stalks celery, cut fine
2 tablespoons drained French capers or ⅓ jar Italian salted ones soaked overnight and then drained
1 small jar stuffed Spanish olives, with sweet peppers (about 4½ to 6-oz. jar)

1 tablespoon sugar
1 tablespoon vinegar
Salt, pepper

Brown the chicken and garlic in the olive oil. Add tomatoes, tomato paste, celery, onion, sugar, vinegar, capers, olives cut in half, salt and pepper, and almost enough water to cover if there is not sufficient juice on the tomatoes. Simmer over a low heat for 2 hours or until tender. Serve hot with a bowl of flaky, fluffy rice. Serves 6.

CHICKEN CASHEW

1 chicken (2½ to 3½ lbs.), ready to cook
1 teaspoon salt
1 rib celery
1 cup ground cashew nuts
¼ teaspoon sage
1½ teaspoons salt
⅛ teaspoon pepper
2 tablespoons chopped parsley
1 cup heavy cream
1½ tablespoons sherry
½ cup bread crumbs

Boil chicken with salt and celery until tender, approximately 50 minutes to one hour. Cool, remove meat, and dice. Into a greased casserole put ½ cup ground cashews, then a layer of chicken. Sprinkle with salt, pepper, sage and parsley. Add another layer of nuts and chicken, then remaining seasonings. Pour over this the cream and sherry. Top with bread crumbs and a few broken cashews. Bake in oven preheated to 325° until top is browned, about 25 to 30 minutes. Serves 4 to 6.

CHICKEN BREASTS BEDDED DOWN ON A PURÉE OF FRESH PEAS

8 chicken breasts
3 tablespoons butter
4 cups cooked puréed fresh peas (about 2
    packages of frozen peas, cooked and
    put through a sieve)
1 small onion, chopped fine
3 eggs, separated
2 tablespoons rum
Salt, pepper

Either sauté the chicken breasts slowly in the butter until brown on both sides, cover and cook over a very low flame until tender, or roast in the oven at 350° with the butter, basting from time to time for about 15 minutes or until the chicken is tender. Mix the puréed peas with the onion, egg yolks, rum, salt and pepper. Fold in gently the stiffly beaten egg whites and spread on a large, shallow baking dish. Arrange the chicken breasts on the top of it; they will sink slightly to the bottom and be halfway covered with a soufflélike mixture. Bake in a medium oven 45 to 50 minutes or until the purée part is puffy and brown. Serves 4 generously.

CHICKEN CASSEROLE WITH CELERY

1 3-lb. chicken, cut up as for frying
1½ teaspoons salt
1 medium-sized onion
1 cup chopped celery
1 8-oz. package egg noodles
1 10½-oz. can condensed cream-of-mushroom
    soup
1 cup buttered bread crumbs

Cook chicken, celery and onions in about 3 cups of water for about an hour. Remove meat from bones and chop fine. Strain stock. Add noodles to stock and cook 8 minutes. Drain liquid from noodles and set aside. Combine chopped chicken and noodles in mixing bowl. To mushroom soup add enough stock to make 3 cups, and season with 1½ teaspoons salt. Add soup-stock mixture to chicken and noodles and mix. Place mixture in a greased casserole and sprinkle with buttered crumbs. Bake 30 minutes at 350°. Serves 6.

CHICKEN IN CUCUMBER SAUCE

Something somewhat new and somewhat different, yet simple.

> 1 cup sour cream
> 1 cucumber, peeled and diced
> 1 chicken (about 2½ to 3 lbs.), cut up
>   as for frying
> ½ cup bacon drippings
> 1 medium-sized onion, chopped fine
> Salt, pepper

Mix the cucumber and sour cream together and let stand for an hour or more so that the sour cream will absorb the flavor of the cucumber. Brown the chicken on all sides in the bacon fat in a heavy iron skillet. Add the chopped onion, salt and pepper, cook until the onion is pale yellow, then add the sour cream and cucumber. Cover pan tightly and cook over a very low heat until tender, which should be from 30 to 45 minutes. Serve in the sauce with *kasha* or brown rice and a tomato aspic salad to accompany it. Hot corn bread goes well with this too. The sour cream will separate slightly in the cooking, but don't let that bother you—it is as it should be. Serves 4.

CHICKEN CASSEROLE WITH SAGE BISCUITS

Surprisingly different, surprisingly good.

> 1 2½ to 3½-lb. chicken, cut up
> Salt
> Pepper
> ½ teaspoon monosodium glutamate
> Kitchen Bouquet
> ¾ cup lard or other shortening
> 1½ cups prepared biscuit mix
> ¾ teaspoon sage
> ¼ teaspoon dried parsley (1 teaspoon fresh)
> ½ cup milk
> 1 tablespoon flour

Shake salt and pepper lightly over each piece of chicken. Dust lightly with monosodium glutamate and brush with Kitchen Bouquet. Have the fat medium hot in frying pan and cook chicken until lightly browned. Add sage, parsley and enough milk to biscuit mix to form stiff dough. Roll ½ inch thick and cut into desired shape. Place fried chicken in casserole dish. Cover with thin brown gravy made by adding the tablespoon of flour to drippings in frying pan and thinning with small amount of water. Place cutout dough on top and bake at 450° until dough is brown, about 25 minutes. Serves 4 to 5.

CHICKEN IN CORN MEAL BATTER PUDDING WITH SALT PORK GRAVY

> 1 2½ to 3-lb. chicken, cut up as for frying
> ¼ cup butter
> Salt, pepper
> 1 package corn-bread ready-mix, mixed
> according to directions

¼ lb. salt pork or fat back, diced and
    soaked in ice water
2 tablespoons flour
1 cup milk
  Salt, pepper
3 slices crumbled cooked bacon

Sauté the chicken in the fat until brown on all sides, then arrange in the bottom of a shallow buttered casserole. Pour the corn-bread mixture on top and bake in a 375° oven 20 to 25 minutes or until the top is browned and shrunk from the sides. Meanwhile, make the gravy. Sauté the cubes of pork—dried first, of course—and drain on paper towels. Pour off all but 2 tablespoons of the pork fat and stir in the flour. Cook over a low flame until well blended. Add the milk slowly, stirring until thickened and smooth, then add the cooked pork cubes and the cooked bacon. Put in a bowl and serve with the chicken-batter pudding. Serves 4.

CHICKEN IN MUSHROOM SAUCE

1 chicken (2½ lbs.), cut up as for frying
3 tablespoons butter
  Salt, pepper
1 10½-oz. can condensed cream-of-mushroom
    soup
½ cup milk or cream
¼ cup sherry

Sauté the chicken in the butter until brown on all sides. Transfer to a casserole, sprinkle with salt and pepper and add the mushroom soup, which has been diluted with the milk and sherry. Bake in a 350° oven for about 1 hour or until tender. Serves 2 to 3.

CHICKEN PIE WITH SWEET POTATO CRUST

A combination beloved by most Southerners—and many Northerners, after they get used to the idea.

> 2 cups diced or sliced chicken
> 1 No. 2 can small boiled onions, drained—
> but save the juice
> 2 green peppers, seeds removed and sliced thin
> ⅓ cup finely chopped parsley
> 2 tablespoons butter
> 2 tablespoons flour
> 2 cups chicken broth
> 1 teaspoon grated lemon peel
> Salt, pepper

Chicken Pie:

Put a layer of chicken in the baking dish, a layer of green pepper and then a layer of onions. Sprinkle generously with the parsley and repeat until all the ingredients are used. Make a thin sauce by melting the butter, blending in the flour and adding the chicken broth slowly, stirring until thickened and smooth. Add the lemon peel, salt and pepper, and pour over the chicken. Top with sweet-potato crust made this way:

> 1 cup mashed sweet potato (canned may
> be used, just mash with a fork)
> ¼ cup melted butter
> 1 egg
> 1 tablespoon grated orange peel, unless
> you use the frozen concentrate

1 tablespoon orange juice (or 2 tablespoons
  undiluted frozen concentrated orange
  juice)
1 cup sifted flour
1 teaspoon baking powder
½ teaspoon salt

Sift the flour with the baking powder and add to the sweet potato, which has been mixed with the butter, the egg and the orange. Roll about ¼ inch thick, to fit the top of the casserole, pinch on and bake in a 350° oven for about 40 minutes. Serves 6.

CHICKEN POTPIE

1 chicken (3½ to 5 lbs.), cut in pieces
4 or 5 large potatoes, peeled and cut in
  thick slices
3 large onions, also cut in thick slices
  Salt, pepper
  Recipe for 2-crust-pie dough made according
    to a good basic recipe or from a ready-mix,
    rolled and cut into 2-inch squares

Wash the pieces of chicken and pat dry. Put a layer of chicken in the bottom of a Dutch oven or deep enameled ironware casserole. Cover with a layer of potato slices and then a layer of onion slices and squares of the pie dough. Repeat until all ingredients are used but make sure that the top layer is of pie dough. Add water up to about halfway. Cover the pot tightly and cook over a very low flame until the chicken is tender, about 1½ hours. Serves 4 to 6.

CHICKEN-RICE CASSEROLE CALIFORNIA

4 tablespoons butter
5 tablespoons flour
1 cup rich milk or evaporated milk
½ cup chicken stock (canned or bouillon-cube broth may be used)
½ cup California sauterne or other white table wine
1 teaspoon celery salt
Salt and pepper to taste
2 cups diced cooked or canned chicken
3 cups cooked rice (1 cup uncooked)
¼ cup minced pimiento
1 4-oz. can mushroom stems and pieces, drained
½ cup slivered blanched almonds
Buttered fine bread crumbs
Paprika

Melt butter and stir in flour; add milk, chicken stock and wine. Cook, stirring constantly, until the mixture boils and thickens. Add seasoning. Combine chicken, rice, pimiento, mushrooms, almonds and sauce, and mix lightly. Turn into a buttered casserole; sprinkle with bread crumbs and paprika. Bake in a moderately hot oven, 375°, for about 25 minutes or until bubbly and delicately browned. Serves 6.

CHICKEN SAUTÉ IN ONION SAUCE

1 chicken (about 3½ lbs.), cut up for frying
2 tablespoons butter
2 tablespoons olive oil
3 tablespoons flour

1¼ cups onion soup (homemade, canned or
   made from dehydrated mix)
½ cup California sauterne or other white
   table wine
½ teaspoon Worcestershire sauce
   Salt and pepper

Brown the chicken in the butter and olive oil, which have
been heated together. Remove the chicken and drain.
Blend the flour with the liquid and add onion soup, wine,
Worcestershire sauce, salt and pepper. Cook, stirring constantly, until the mixture boils and thickens, and return
chicken to the sauce. Cover and cook slowly for about 45
minutes or until the chicken is tender, basting occasionally. Serves 3 or 4.

CHICKEN WITH CORN

A contemporary version of an old Southern dish. Made
this way, it's in the lower brackets of time and money and
pleasantly rewarding. Naturally if you wish to sauté your
chicken first and then grate corn kernels from fresh ears
of corn, it is even more rewarding.

1 1-lb. can chicken fricassee (the kind with
   gravy and lots of good chicken fat)
1 can (about 16 ozs.) whole-kernel corn
   Salt, lots of freshly ground black pepper
2 tablespoons butter

Arrange the fricassee in the bottom of the casserole and
spread the corn on top, drained, if it's the sloshy kind.
Sprinkle with salt and quite a lot of the black pepper. Dot
with pieces of the butter and bake in a 350° oven about 20
minutes or until thoroughly hot. Serves 2.

CHICKEN TETRAZZINI

1 boiled chicken (cook according to basic
    instructions, and remove meat from
    bones and cut into fine pieces)
½ lb. spaghetti
    Chicken broth (from boiling the chicken)
½ lb. mushrooms, sliced; or, to be lavish, 1 lb.
    3 tablespoons butter
    3 more tablespoons butter
    3 tablespoons flour
    2 cups chicken broth
    1 cup heavy cream
    3 tablespoons sherry
    Salt, pepper
½ cup grated Parmesan cheese or Swiss
    and Parmesan cheeses mixed

Cook the spaghetti in boiling-hot chicken broth until barely tender but not squashy. Drain and keep warm. Be sure
to keep 2 cups of broth for the sauce. To do this add some
water to the broth used for cooking the spaghetti, if necessary. Sauté the mushrooms in butter—the first 3 tablespoons of butter—until tender, about 3 to 5 minutes. Make
a sauce by melting the additional butter, adding the flour
and stirring in the broth ever so slowly! Heat the cream
and add it, with the sherry and seasonings, to the sauce.
To ½ of the sauce add the chicken. To the other ½ portion add the well-drained spaghetti and mushrooms. Put
the spaghetti-and-mushroom part into a baking dish,
whirling it around the side and leaving a well in the center. Pour the chicken mixture in the center and sprinkle
the whole dish with the grated cheese. Bake in a 350°
oven until lightly browned, about 10 to 12 minutes, and
serve right from the baking dish. Serves 8 to 10.

COQ AU VIN

This version of the classic dish is from Marcel Perret of the Café St. Denis on East 53rd Street, New York. According to classic principles this must always be made with a rooster or cockerel, but Marcel says that roosters in this country are apt to be aged and tough and besides, buying pre-packaged chickens, as so many do these days, it is not easy to identify their sex.

> 2 broilers (2½ lbs. each), split in halves
> Salt, pepper
> 2 onions, diced
> 2 carrots, diced
> 3 bay leaves
> 2 stalks celery, cut in 1-inch pieces
> Burgundy to cover
> Flour
> ¼ cup butter

Put the halves of chicken, salt, pepper, onion, carrots, bay leaves and celery into a bowl and cover with red wine. Let stand for 3 or 4 days in the refrigerator. When ready to cook take the pieces of chicken out of the marinade and dry them thoroughly with a towel. Sprinkle all over very lightly with flour. Put butter into skillet and heat it until it is a nice brown. Drop the halves of chicken into it and turn them around and around until they are very well browned, then transfer the chicken to a cocotte with a cover or a Dutch oven. Add the marinade with the carrots, celery, bay leaves and onion and let it cook over a low fire until it is done and the marinade has been reduced to a rich, dark sauce. Sometimes the lid should be lifted slightly off center to allow the steam to escape. Transfer the pieces of chicken to a warm hot platter, strain the sauce and pour over it. Serves 4 generously.

CHICKEN, VEAL AND HAM CASSEROLE

1 chicken (2½ to 3½ lbs.), cut up for
   fricassee or frying
   Giblets and neck
½ lb. uncooked veal, diced
½ lb. uncooked ham, diced
1 bunch carrots, scraped and sliced
8 to 12 small onions, peeled, or 1 No. 2 can
   small boiled onions and the juice
3 cups chicken broth
1 cup white wine
1 jigger cognac
1 piece bay leaf
½ teaspoon thyme
   Salt, pepper

Put all the ingredients, except wine and cognac, in a Dutch oven with 3 cups chicken broth, and simmer over a low flame about 1½ hours or until tender, adding the wine and cognac after about 1 hour. Skim off the fat while hot by blotting with paper towels or chill and remove the fat. Reheat; serve with the unthickened juices and French bread for dunking. Serves 4 generously.

CHICKEN WITH NOODLES

A gentle, bland dish.

2 cups diced cooked chicken
3 tablespoons butter
3 tablespoons flour
2 cups milk
   Salt, pepper

1 package noodles (the spinach ones are
    prettiest)
Finely chopped parsley and/or finely
    grated Swiss or Parmesan cheese

Make a sauce by melting the butter and blending in the flour. When cooked sufficiently to be rid of the floury taste, add the milk slowly and stir until smooth and thickened. Add salt and pepper and chicken. Meanwhile, cook the noodles in boiling salted water until tender but not mushy. Drain and arrange in a casserole, pour the chicken mixture on top and sprinkle with the parsley and/or cheese. Bake in a 350° oven for 15 to 20 minutes. Serves 4.

CHICKEN WITH OKRA

1 chicken (2½ lbs.)
2 tablespoons butter
2 medium-sized onions, sliced thin
1 lb. fresh okra (small pods left whole, just
    stems cut off, older ones sliced)
1 green pepper, seeds removed and pepper
    coarsely diced
2 cups chicken stock
  Juice of ½ lemon
  Salt, pepper
  More salt and pepper

Sauté the chicken in the butter until golden brown on all sides. Arrange the chicken in a deep casserole with a lid. Add the sliced onions and the okra and green pepper. Pour in the chicken broth, lemon juice, salt and pepper. Cover and cook in a 350° oven until tender. Serves 3 or 4. Accompany with a bowl of hot rice, corn muffins and a good green salad.

COMPANY CHICKEN CASSEROLE

This dish has everything: the rich flavor of crisp, fried chicken; the delicacy of a soufflé; a brown, flaky crust; and a creamy, bacony flavor.

> 1 chicken (3 to 3½ lbs.), cut up for frying
> ¼ cup flour
> 1 teaspoon salt
> ¼ teaspoon black pepper
> ½ cup cooking oil or shortening

Batter:

> 1½ cups sifted flour
> 1½ teaspoons baking powder
> 1 teaspoon salt
> 4 eggs
> 1½ cups milk
> 3 tablespoons melted butter

Keep the wings, back, neck and giblets for soup. Mix the flour, salt and pepper and coat the meaty pieces of chicken with it. Brown them in hot shortening in a heavy pan. Drain chicken on paper towels. Save the drippings in the pan for gravy.

Set oven at 350°. Sift flour, baking powder and salt together. Beat eggs until very light, then stir in milk and melted butter. Stir the egg mixture into dry ingredients slowly, to prevent flour from lumping. Then beat batter with egg beater until smooth. Pour into greased, heavy 10-inch baking dish or casserole that is 3 inches deep. Arrange pieces of browned chicken on top. Bake 1 hour or until batter is puffy and brown. Serve with gravy.

Gravy:

2½ tablespoons drippings left
from browning chicken
2 cups water
3 tablespoons flour
Salt, pepper
3 slices cooked, crumbled bacon

Add the 2 cups water to drippings in pan and stir up all the browned particles. Bring to a boil. Blend flour with ½ cup cold water, then pour into boiling liquid while stirring vigorously to prevent lumps. Add the bacon. Simmer 3 or 4 minutes. Season with salt and pepper.

HAM AND CHICKEN PIE WITH OYSTERS

2 cups cooked chicken, sliced
½ lb. cooked ham, sliced (the slices
cut in quarters)
1 pint oysters
3 cups chicken gravy made according to the
basic recipe but including the oyster
liquor as part of the liquid
Pie dough for 1 crust

Arrange in a casserole the chicken, ham, oysters in layers, repeating until all the ingredients are used. Pour in the gravy and top with the pie dough. Pinch closed around the edges and brush the crust with milk. Bake in a 450° oven until the pie crust is brown and cooked and the meat good and hot. Serves 4.

CHICKEN TUFOLI

This is a slightly involved dish which may be prepared ahead so that there is no last-minute fuss. The tufoli is one of the largest if not the largest of the *pasta*.

    ½ lb. tufoli
    2 cups diced chicken, cooked or canned
    2 raw eggs
    ⅓ cup freshly grated Parmesan cheese
    2 tablespoons capers, drained
    1 clove garlic, minced
    2 small onions or 1 large onion, chopped fine
    3 tablespoons olive oil
    1 can Italian tomato paste
    1 No. 2 can tomatoes
      Salt, pepper

Cook the tufoli in a large amount of salted boiling water until tender but not squashy. Remove from the water and drain. Mix the chopped chicken with the egg, cheese, capers, salt and pepper, and stuff with your fingers or a spoon into the drained, slightly cooled tufoli. Arrange in a baking dish and make a marinara sauce by cooking the onion and garlic in the olive oil until pale yellow, and then adding the tomato paste and tomatoes and cooking until rich and thick. The time will vary according to your patience. The Italians cook it a very long time but Americans are apt to get impatient after a ½ or ¾ of an hour and consider the project completed. Pour over the stuffed tufoli and bake in a 350° oven until thoroughly hot, 25 to 30 minutes. Serve with a salad and some Italian bread. Serves 4.

CREAMED CHICKEN WITH BISCUIT TOP

    2 cups coarsely chopped cooked chicken
    1 cup chopped cooked celery
    ½ cup mushrooms
    2 cups thickened chicken stock or 2 cups
        medium white sauce (made with 3
        tablespoons butter, 3 tablespoons flour
        and 2 cups milk)
    Salt and pepper to taste

Combine ingredients and pour into greased 1½-quart casserole. Place biscuits on top and bake in hot oven, 450°, for 15 to 20 minutes.

Biscuits:

    2 cups sifted enriched flour
    3 teaspoons baking powder
    Salt
    2 to 4 tablespoons shortening
    ⅔ to ¾ cup milk

Sift together flour, baking powder and salt. Cut or rub in shortening. Add milk to make a soft dough. Turn out onto lightly floured board and knead gently 30 seconds. Roll out ½ inch thick. Cut with floured biscuit cutter and place on top of chicken concoction. Bake in hot oven, 450°, for 15 to 20 minutes. Serve with additional hot biscuits. Makes 4 servings.

OVEN CREAMED CHICKEN

1 chicken (2½ to 3 lbs.), cut in quarters
  Salt, pepper
3 tablespoons butter
3 more tablespoons butter
3 tablespoons flour
2 cups milk
  More salt
2 tablespoons finely chopped parsley
2 tablespoons finely chopped celery
¼ cup sherry

Soak the chicken in ice water for an hour, though naturally it will not be ice water that long a time. This keeps the meat juicy. Drain it, pat dry and sprinkle with salt and pepper. Dot generously with 3 tablespoons of butter. Put in a shallow casserole that has a lid, but roast uncovered in the open pan in a 350° oven for 15 minutes. Make a sauce by melting the additional butter in a saucepan, blending in the flour and adding the milk slowly. Add salt and cook until thickened, stirring constantly. Add the parsley, celery and sherry and pour over the chicken. Cover casserole and bake in a 300° oven until the chicken is tender, which is usually about ½ hour. Serves 4.

PIERRE'S CHICKEN CHASSEUR

As served at Pierre's Restaurant in New York.

1 chicken (2½ to 3 lbs.), cut up as for frying
1 large onion, sliced thin
1 lb. fresh mushrooms, sliced (save stems
    for broth or sauce)
¼ lb. butter or ½ cup shortening

1 small bay leaf
1 small clove garlic, peeled
    Salt, pepper
½ cup dry white wine
2 lbs. tomatoes, peeled, seeded and chopped
    or 1 No. 2 or No. 2½ can tomatoes

Melt the butter or shortening. Add salt and pepper to chicken, dust lightly with flour and cook 5 minutes in the butter until golden brown. Add onion, mushrooms, bay leaf and garlic. Cook 10 minutes until all brown. Add wine, then tomatoes. Cover and simmer about 25 minutes. Total cooking time is about 40 minutes. If you wish more sauce, add more tomatoes. Serve with noodles, rice or potatoes. Serves 4.

THELMA'S MILK CHICKEN

This is surprisingly simple and surpassingly good.

1 chicken (3½ to 5 lbs.), cut up as for frying
    Flour, salt, pepper
    Milk

Dredge the chicken lightly, paper-bag method, in flour seasoned with salt and pepper. Put in a deep casserole and cover with milk (this amount will vary, of course, according to the size of the chicken and the casserole). Bake in a 350° oven for ½ hour; then, with a fork and tongs or two forks, put the brown top pieces on the bottom and the pale bottom pieces on top. Add more milk, if necessary, to keep the liquid about the top, and bake for 1 hour more or until the chicken is very tender and the milk has cooked down to a wonderful sauce. Remove the pieces of chicken to a warm platter and strain the sauce over it before serving. Serves 4.

POULET GRATINE

One of Ali Bab's recipes that he might or might not recognize.

1 chicken (about 2½ lbs.), cut up as for frying
3 tablespoons butter
1 tablespoon flour
1 pint heavy cream
　Salt and pepper
2 whole eggs, 2 egg yolks
⅓ cup finely grated Parmesan or Gruyère
　cheese, or a mixture of the two
　Bread crumbs

Sauté the chicken in the butter until it is a pretty brown, and then make a paste of the flour and some of the cream. Pour over the chicken, add salt and pepper and cook slowly until tender. Remove from the fire. Transfer the chicken to a shallow warm casserole. Pour the cream and juices from the pan slowly on the beaten eggs and egg yolks, and then pour back over the chicken. Sprinkle the top of the chicken generously with the cheese and bread crumbs and, if possible, put under a broiler until brown. If not, put in a 400° oven for 15 minutes. Serves 4.

TERRAPINED CHICKEN

This recipe, still workable and good, is from the *Carbondale Cook Book* of tried and tested recipes prepared by the young lady workers of the Methodist Episcopal Church of Carbondale, Pennsylvania. (Third edition, revised and enlarged, 1903.) The quantities are rather large as it is intended to serve 25 people. It is a good buffet dish for those who like a party that size, served with a good ham, a salad and, of course, some hot bread.

"Three pints of cold boiled chicken. Three hard-boiled eggs, three heaping tablespoons of flour that have been browned in the oven, half a pint of chicken stock, one pint of milk, one even teaspoon of salt, a pinch of cayenne, one half teaspoon of mace, a large lump of butter (a heaping tablespoon). Mince the chicken fine, rub the eggs through a fine sieve, melt the butter in a large stewpan and add the flour; next add the stock and milk which has been scalded, the chicken in which all the seasoning has been well mixed, and eggs. Cook slowly a half hour. This is to be served on brown toast and will serve 25 persons."

SCALLOPED CHICKEN

This is another recipe from the *Carbondale Cook Book*— tried and tested recipes prepared by the young lady workers of the Methodist Episcopal Church of Carbondale, Pennsylvania. (Third edition, revised and enlarged, 1903.)

The amounts are purposely vague and so are the amounts of leftovers, but the recipe works in almost any reasonable proportions.

"Cut in small pieces the meat from the remains of cold roast chicken. Put the bones, fat, skin and gristle in a saucepan and nearly cover with cold water, and cook slowly for a gravy. Cover bottom of a baking dish with fine bread crumbs and bits of butter, then fill with the chicken and season. A few oysters placed in alternate layers with the chicken is a great improvement; spread crumbs over the top. When all the good from the bones is in the gravy, strain and thicken and use nearly a cupful over the scallop. Invert a plate over the baking dish and place in a hot oven. After the gravy bubbles, remove the plate and brown the top."

SCALLOPED CHICKEN WITH OYSTER PLANT

Through ignorance and misuse oyster plant, which can be quite delicate and delicious, has acquired a bad name. Properly cooked it has an elusive flavor somewhat like oysters.

> 1 bunch oyster plant (which is to say, salsify)
> Flour
> 3 tablespoons butter
> 3 tablespoons flour
> 1 cup chicken broth
> 1 cup cream
> ⅓ cup Parmesan or Switzerland Swiss cheese, freshly grated
> Salt, pepper
> 2 cups diced cooked or canned chicken
> 2 tablespoons chopped chives (these can now be bought successfully dried so that they hold their color and flavor)

Scrape and slice the oyster plant immediately into 3 or 4 cups water with 1 or 2 tablespoons flour to prevent discoloring. Simmer until just barely tender, 7 to 15 minutes, and remove immediately from the fire and drain. Oyster plant cooked too long becomes tough again. Meanwhile, make a cheese sauce by blending the butter with the flour and adding the broth slowly, stirring until thickened and smooth. Then add the cream, salt, pepper and the cheese, and stir until melted.

Arrange a layer of the sliced cooked oyster plant in a casserole, then a layer of the chicken, then the cheese sauce. Sprinkle with chives and repeat until all the ingredients are used. Put in a 350° oven briefly to brown and heat. Serves 4.

INDIVIDUAL CHICKEN PIES

1 4 to 5-lb. chicken, boiled or pressure cooked
according to basic instructions
2 batches of pie dough, mixed according to
basic recipe or from a ready-mix
4 ozs. salt pork, chopped fine and parboiled
1 No. 2 can small boiled onions or about 12
small white onions parboiled
1 small can (or ⅓ Chinese can) water
chestnuts, drained and sliced thin
⅓ cup finely chopped parsley

Chicken Gravy:

3 tablespoons butter
3 tablespoons flour
2 cups chicken broth
Salt, pepper

Line 6 individual deep casseroles with the pie dough and put in several layers of white and dark meat. Divide the salt pork into 6 parts, put a spoonful in each pie, divide the onions into 6 parts, and add with the sliced water chestnuts to each pie. Melt the butter, blend in the flour and add the chicken broth, stirring until smooth and thickened. Add salt and pepper and pour some into each pie dish. Place a circle of pie dough on top, crimp the edges and make a few slashes to allow the steam to escape. Bake in a 400° oven until the crust is brown. Serves 6.

SAUTÉED CHICKEN PROVENÇALE

Another recipe from the Café St. Denis in New York.

> 1 frying chicken (1½ to 2 lbs.), quartered
> Flour
> ¼ cup butter
> 2 cups potatoes, cut in balls or, more traditionally, olive-shape
> ¼ lb. mushrooms, sliced
> 3 shallots, chopped fine
> 1 clove garlic, minced
> 3 tablespoons finely chopped parsley
> Salt, pepper
> ¼ cup white wine
> ¼ cup chicken broth

Bone the quarters of chicken by slitting at the back with a knife and removing the bones as carefully as possible. Flour lightly and brown in the butter on each side for 6 or 8 minutes. Transfer to a shallow baking dish and bake for 10 minutes in a 400° oven surrounded by the potatoes, which have been parboiled and rolled in the hot butter that the chicken was sautéed in. Sauté in the same skillet the mushrooms, shallots and garlic. Add salt and pepper and, just before removing from the stove, mix in the wine and broth. Pour over the potatoes and sprinkle with parsley. Serves 2 or 3.

4

Chicken Livers and Giblets

CHICKEN LIVER PASTE

½ lb. chicken livers
¼ lb. fresh mushrooms
3 tablespoons butter
　Salt, pepper
1 teaspoon grated onion
1 teaspoon lemon juice

Sauté the livers in 1½ tablespoons of butter for about 5 to
8 minutes or until just barely tender. Chop fine, mashing
slightly. Sauté the mushrooms in the additional butter
for about 3 to 5 minutes and chop fine. Mix the mashed
chicken liver with the chopped mushrooms, salt, pepper,
onion and lemon juice. Makes about 2 cups. Serve hot or
cold on thin slices of pumpernickel—not toast or biscuits.

CHICKEN GIBLET PÂTÉ

Slightly more robust than the all-chicken-liver *pâté* and, of course, more frugal.

> 3 sets chicken giblets and necks
> 2 slices onion, 1 minced fine
>   Salt, pepper
> 3 tablespoons butter
> 1 tablespoon cognac

Put all the giblets and necks, except the chicken livers, into 2 cups of cold water with 1 slice of onion and some salt and pepper; cook until all are tender. Meanwhile, briefly but thoroughly sauté the chicken livers in the butter with the minced slice of onion and add a little salt and pepper to them.

Drain the giblets and the necks and pull the meat off the necks. Put it through the meat grinder with the giblets, using the coarsest blade. Add the chicken livers, which have been mashed with a fork, and onion and butter with which they have been cooked. Mix into a paste by adding the cognac and a little of the liquid that the giblets were cooked in and some more melted butter, if necessary, to make the paste smooth. Serve with hot French bread or toast.

CHICKEN GIBLET RICE FROM EGYPT

> 4 sets giblets and necks
> 1 thick slice lemon
> 1 clove garlic, 1 celery stalk and a few
>   celery leaves
> ¼ cup pine nuts or pignolias (almonds
>   could be used)

½ cup butter
½ cup seedless raisins
½ cup butter
4 or more cups chicken broth
2 cups uncooked rice
1 or more teaspoons salt
¼ teaspoon pepper

Simmer giblets and necks in water with lemon slice, garlic, celery and celery leaves. Cook until tender when pricked with a fork, about 1½ hours. Remove neck meat from bones. Trim and chop giblets coarsely. Brown nuts in 2 tablespoons butter; add raisins and giblets. Meanwhile, place remaining butter, broth and rice, which has been washed thoroughly, in a large pot. Add giblet and nut sauce and season to taste. Cover tightly and steam over low heat until rice is tender, fluffy and almost dry, about 15 minutes. Taste for seasoning. Serves 8.

CHICKEN LIVER CUSTARD

1 lb. chicken livers
¼ lb. mushrooms, sliced thin
3 tablespoons butter
8 eggs, beaten
1 cup heavy cream, scalded
Salt, pepper

Sauté the chicken livers and the mushrooms briefly in the butter, then cut the chicken livers into small pieces. Divide the chicken livers and mushrooms and place in 4 individual baking dishes. Add the scalded cream to the beaten eggs and pour ¼ of the mixture over each dish of chicken livers. Bake in a 350° oven for about 25 minutes. Serves 4.

CHICKEN LIVER RISOTTO

A classic Italian dish that is fine for American ways of living, eating and cooking. The chicken livers may be frozen and kept on hand in the freezer and the rice needs no peeling or other tedious preparation. It is filling but not too filling, and the over-all procedure takes something like 25 to 30 minutes.

>   1 cup rice
>   ¼ cup butter
>   2 cups chicken broth
>   Another ¼ cup butter
>   1 lb. chicken livers, cut in pieces
>   ½ lb. mushrooms, sliced
>   Salt, pepper
>   2 tomatoes
>   2 tablespoons finely chopped parsley

Cook the rice in the butter until pale yellow. Add the chicken broth, bring to a boil, cover and turn the heat down very low. Cook for 15 minutes, after which time turn off the heat, remove the lid and run a fork through 2 or 3 times to fluff up the grains. Meanwhile, sauté the chicken livers and mushrooms in the additional butter and add the salt and pepper. This will take about 5 or 10 minutes. Arrange the rice on a deep, small warm platter and spread the chicken liver and mushroom mixture over the hot rice. Take a ricer and put in the 2 tomatoes peeled and seeded. Squeeze over the top of the chicken liver. Strew the parsley over the top. Serves 4.

CHICKEN LIVERS EN BROCHETTE

With this dish you need some comparatively short skewers, about 8 or 10 inches in length. Allow 1 to a customer and slide the meat from the skewer onto each plate when serving, and put the skewers aside.

>1 lb. chicken livers
>4 strips bacon, cut in 1-inch pieces
>½ lb. mushroom caps (save the stems for
>broth and another day)
>Melted butter
>Salt, pepper

Arrange the livers on a skewer, putting first the liver, then a square of bacon, then a mushroom cap, then a liver and so on. Do not pack the skewers too tightly or they will not broil evenly. Brush them with the melted butter and sprinkle with salt and pepper. Put about 3 inches under a broiler on a sheet of aluminum foil—that is, if you dislike cleaning a broiler as much as I do—and broil 3 to 5 minutes on each side. Serves 4.

CHICKEN LIVERS EN BROCHETTE, DEEP FRIED

1 lb. chicken livers
3 or 4 slices bacon cut in pieces
1 egg beaten
  Salt, pepper
1 tablespoon cognac
  Bread crumbs
  Deep fat for frying

Arrange the chicken livers on 4 metal skewers, alternating the pieces of chicken liver with the pieces of bacon. Dip in the egg mixture or brush it on, so that all the pieces are covered, and then roll in the bread crumbs. Lower into fat heated to 365° for 1 to 2 minutes or until golden brown. Drain on paper towels and put in the oven briefly to dry out. To serve, slide the food from each skewer onto a piece of hot buttered toast. Serves 4.

CHICKEN LIVER SOUFFLÉ

½ lb. chicken livers
1 tablespoon finely chopped onion
2 tablespoons butter
3 slices crumbled cooked bacon
3 more tablespoons butter
3 tablespoons flour
1 cup milk or chicken broth
3 eggs, separated
  Salt, pepper

Sauté the chicken livers with the onion in the 2 tablespoons butter. Mash slightly with a fork and add the bacon. Melt the 3 other tablespoons butter in another pan, stir in the flour and blend well. Add the milk or chicken broth and stir constantly until thickened and smooth. Remove from the fire. Add the chicken-livers-and-bacon mixture and egg yolks. Fold in the stiffly beaten egg whites and turn into a greased baking dish with straight sides. Bake in a 350° oven 45 to 50 minutes or until the top is delicately brown and springs back when gently touched. Serves 4.

CURRIED GIBLETS AND CHICKEN WINGS IN CREOLE SAUCE

This is a savory meal for a frugal night.

> 1 clove garlic
> 1 medium-sized onion, chopped fine
> 1 green pepper, chopped and seeds removed
> 3 tablespoons olive oil
> 2 tablespoons or less, depending on taste,
>   good strong curry powder
> Salt
> 1 No. 2½ can tomatoes
> 1 set giblets and neck (from the boiled fowl
>   in the Chicken Management)
> Wings (also from the Chicken Management)
> 1 cup uncooked rice

Sauté the garlic, onion and pepper in the olive oil; add the curry powder, salt, tomatoes, pieces of chicken wings and giblets. Cover and simmer over a low flame while the rice is cooking. Put the rice in 2 cups water with 1 teaspoon salt, bring to a boil, cover, turn flame low and cook 14 minutes. Serve with the curried creole sauce and chicken poured on top. Accompany with plenty of good hot rolls, a salad and a fairly substantial dessert. Serves 4 lightly.

CHICKEN LIVERS AND MUSHROOM CAPS IN WINE SAUCE

A light and delicate dish.

> 1 lb. chicken livers, cut in halves
> 16 to 20 good mushroom caps, depending on size
>   Melted butter
> 2 more tablespoons butter
> 3 tablespoons flour
> 1½ cups strong good chicken broth (that means no bouillon cubes—which are good but weak)
> ½ cup dry white wine
>   Salt, paprika

Brush the chicken livers and the mushroom caps with the melted butter and put under a broiler briefly. The chicken livers will take 5 to 8 minutes, including both sides, and the mushroom caps 3 to 5 minutes. It's up to you whether you want to put them in at the same time and snatch the mushrooms out before the chicken livers or put them in after the chicken livers and take them out at the same time.

Arrange 4 or 5 mushroom caps, depending on how many you bought, in each of 4 individual au gratin dishes, preferably something pretty like copper. Put 1 piece of chicken liver on each mushroom cap and blanket with sauce made this way: Melt the 2 tablespoons of butter, blend in the flour, add the chicken broth slowly, stirring until thick and smooth. Add the white wine, salt and paprika and cook until that is smooth. Pour over the mushrooms and chicken livers and put in a 350° oven 10 to 15 minutes or until hot and bubbly. Serves 4.

GEORGIA'S CHICKEN LIVERS IN MADEIRA SAUCE

There is no particular virtue to the night air in marinating. It merely means when you are supposed to marinate something overnight that this is a convenient length of time. People that think of these things early in the day can easily start them for dinner.

> 1 lb. chicken livers, cut in large pieces
> 3 tablespoons olive oil
> 1 tablespoon tarragon vinegar
> 1 clove garlic
> ¼ cup Madeira
>   Salt, pepper
>   Pinch of sugar
> 2 tablespoons butter
> 1½ tablespoons flour
> ¾ cup chicken stock or broth
>   Another ¼ cup Madeira
>   Finely shredded or grated peel of 1 orange
>   Fresh-made toast

Marinate the liver overnight in the olive oil, vinegar, salt, pepper, garlic, first ¼ cup of Madeira and sugar. Drain on paper towels. Sauté in the butter and transfer livers to a warm plate. Thicken the juices in the pan by adding the flour mixed with enough water to make a thin paste; then add the chicken stock and second ¼ cup of Madeira, stirring constantly until smooth and thickened. Finally, add the shredded orange peel. The shredding may be done rather simply by peeling a whole orange with a potato peeler and then chopping it very fine, or it may be grated the usual way. Pour over the toast and serve. Serves 4.

CHICKEN LIVERS ON TOAST WITH PÂTÉ

This is very simple and very elegant, especially when you use the imported *pâté de fois gras,* but good whatever kind you use and no matter how redundant it seems to use 2 livers.

> 1 lb. chicken livers, cut in pieces
> 3 tablespoons butter
>   Salt, pepper
> 8 slices freshly toasted white bread
>   *Pâté*
> 2 slices cooked crumbled bacon

Sauté the chicken livers in the butter until tender and pink but not bloody. Add salt and pepper. Spread the toast with the *pâté* and arrange 2 slices on each plate. Sprinkle with some of the crumbled bacon and strew the chicken livers on top, dividing more or less evenly for the 4 plates. Serves 4.

CHOPPED CHICKEN LIVER

One of the simplest and best of all spreads.

> 2 tablespoons chicken fat
> 2 small onions, chopped
> 1 lb. chicken livers
>   Salt, pepper
> 3 or 4 hard-cooked eggs, chopped
>   More chicken fat if necessary

Sauté the onions in the fat until pale yellow. Add the chicken livers and sauté slowly until tender and cooked. Chop the livers and onions very fine with a knife, or put through the coarse blade of a grinder. If necessary add more chicken fat to make the paste moist. Then add the chopped hard-cooked eggs and serve with pumpernickel bread, crackers or Melba toast. Makes about 2 cups.

SPAGHETTI WITH CHICKEN LIVER SAUCE

Tried, true and traditional. Sometimes called Chicken Caruso because of his fondness for this.

    3 tablespoons olive oil
    2 onions, chopped fine
    1 clove garlic, minced
    1 No. 2½ can tomatoes
    1 can Italian tomato paste
    1 tablespoon mixed pickling spice
       Salt, pepper
    ½ to 1 lb. chicken livers, cut in pieces
    ½ lb. spaghetti

Sauté the onion and the garlic in the olive oil until pale yellow and translucent. Add the tomatoes, tomato paste, pickling spice, salt and pepper and let simmer for ½ to ¾ of an hour—the Italians, of course, do this for several hours and it's good, but this seems long enough to humor a sauce in these hurried days. Evaluate your own time.

Just before serving sauté the chicken livers briefly in the butter—briefly means about 5 to 8 minutes—and add the sauce. Cook the spaghetti in boiling water until barely tender, rinse under cold water, and then very quickly dash under hot water. Drain and put on a hot platter. Pour the chicken-liver sauce over the spaghetti and serve with a bowl of fresh-grated Parmesan cheese, to sprinkle over all, and, of course, a good green salad and plenty of Italian bread. Serves 4.

EGGS STUFFED WITH CHICKEN LIVERS

       ½ lb. chicken livers
       8 strips bacon, fried crisp
      10 hard-cooked eggs, halved
       2 tablespoons finely minced parsley
       ½ teaspoon crushed dried tarragon
       ½ teaspoon onion salt
       ¼ teaspoon salt
       1 tablespoon minced chives
       ½ teaspoon black pepper
       3 tablespoons mayonnaise
         Paprika

Boil and mash chicken livers. Crumble bacon. Combine
with mashed yolks scooped out of whites. Blend in remaining ingredients except paprika. Stuff back into white
shells either with a spoon or through a pastry tube. Garnish with sprinkle of paprika. Makes 20 hors d'oeuvres.

HOT CHICKEN LIVER PÂTÉ

There is something so impressive about a hot hors d'oeuvre
that it is best not to tell people just how easily one like
this can be concocted, especially when the livers and the
French bread are kept on hand.

       ½ lb. chicken livers, fresh or frozen
       2 tablespoons sweet butter
         Salt, pepper
       1 tablespoon brandy
       1 loaf freshly baked Pepperidge Farm
           (brown and serve) French bread
         More sweet butter

Sauté the chicken livers very slowly in the butter until

tender but not hard. (In an emergency the frozen livers may be cooked when partially thawed, but they are better when completely thawed and drained.) Mash with a fork, add salt, pepper and brandy. Put in a pottery jar. Cut the warm bread in 1½-inch slices slanting crosswise, and once down the middle lengthwise. Serve with the warm *pâté*, sweet butter and, of course, some knives for spreading. The number this serves depends on what other hors d'oeuvres you are serving and whether the guests are staying for dinner and expect to get fed soon.

SCRAMBLED CHICKEN LIVERS ON TOASTED ENGLISH MUFFINS WITH ANCHOVY

A rich odorous mish-mash.

> 3 tablespoons butter
> ½ lb. chicken livers, cut in pieces
> 6 eggs
> ⅓ cup chili sauce
> Salt, pepper, if necessary
> 4 English muffins, split and toasted
> Anchovy paste

Sauté the chicken livers in the butter until just barely done—which means not running with blood. Break in the eggs, add the chili sauce and a little salt and pepper—depending on how well the chili sauce is seasoned—and stir slowly over a very low flame until the eggs are moist and just barely coagulated. Put 2 halves of the toasted muffin spread with anchovy paste on each plate and pour ¼ of the egg-and-chicken-liver concoction over them. Serve immediately as a late-supper dish, Sunday breakfast or for luncheon. Serves 4.

PIERRE'S PÂTÉ

Blissfully eating *pâté* from restaurant to restaurant in New York is, of course, conducive to obesity. This *pâté*, which is served at Pierre's Restaurant on East 52nd Street, is one of the best of the delicate and bland types.

¼ lb. chicken livers
¼ lb. calves' liver
½ cup milk
½ medium-sized carrot
½ medium-sized onion
¼ lb. lean pork
¼ to ½ teaspoon pickling spices, pounded
¼ to ½ teaspoon salt
1 oz. (by weight) margarine, pork fat or chicken fat
½ cup milk
2½ slices white bread
¼ lb. butter
3 tablespoons (1½ ozs.) sherry
1¾ tablespoons (¾ oz.) brandy
1 can good chicken consommé, reduced to 9 ozs.
1 tablespoon sherry
Little extra salt and pepper
¾ envelope plain gelatin dissolved in a little water

Cut up the calves' liver and chicken livers into small pieces and soak for 2 hours in the ½ cup of milk. Meanwhile, dice the carrot, onion and lean pork and add to them the pickling spices and salt. Heat the margarine, pork fat or chicken fat in a heavy pot with a tight cover, and cook the vegetables, pork and spices, covered, over a very low heat in the melted fat for 2 hours.

Soak the bread in ½ cup milk, drain the livers and combine the drained livers, cooked pork and vegetables with the soaked bread. Put the mixture first through grinder, then through food mill. Melt ¼ lb. butter in a double boiler and add the sieved mixture. Cook for 30 minutes, stirring occasionally to blend the butter and the solids. Cool off over ice, beating, until *pâté* is at room temperature—it will seem lumpy. Whip thoroughly, gradually adding the sherry and brandy, and then refrigerate. When cold, cover with an aspic made of the consommé, 1 tablespoon of sherry, a little salt and gelatin.

Makes about a pint, rather more than 1 lb.

RING MOLD OF RICE WITH CHICKEN LIVERS

1 cup rice
2 cups chicken broth
Salt
3 tablespoons butter
1 lb. chicken livers
3 more tablespoons butter
Salt, pepper
1 jigger sherry

Put the rice in a pan with the chicken broth, add salt and bring to a boil. Cover tightly and cook over a very low heat for 14 minutes. Mix with the melted butter and pack into a 1-pint ring mold. Set the mold in a pan of hot water and bake in a 350° oven for 20 minutes. Loosen the edges with a knife, place a small warm platter over the mold and invert. Fill the center with the chicken livers, which have been sautéed briefly in the butter. Add salt, pepper and sherry to the various juices in the pan and pour over the livers. Serves 4.

GIBLET HASH WITH POACHED EGGS

This is one of the dishes you make with the giblets you
have been putting into the freezing unit from the last 4
chickens you have cooked.

> 4 sets giblets and the necks
> 3 medium-sized potatoes, peeled and diced
> 1 medium-sized onion, chopped
> 2 stalks celery, leaves and all chopped fine
> ½ teaspoon thyme
>   Salt, pepper
> 1 tablespoon butter
> 1 tablespoon flour
> 4 slices fresh-made toast
> 4 poached eggs

Put the giblets, except the livers, into 3 cups of cold salted
water and cook until tender. Remove from the liquid and
cut into small pieces, cutting the meat carefully off the
necks. Cook the potatoes, onion, celery, thyme, salt and
pepper in the liquid until tender. Add the chopped giblets
and the chicken livers, which have been sautéed briefly
in 1 tablespoon butter and then cut up. Thicken the stew
or hash with flour mixed with a little water to a thin paste.
Serve on the toast with a poached egg on top of each
serving. Serves 4.

POACHED EGGS ON CHICKEN GIBLET
PÂTÉ ON TOAST

This may be made with either the giblet *pâté* or the chicken-liver *pâté*. It is fine for those of us who from time to
time must be discreet about our food and go on a modified
bland diet.

8 slices toast, preferably thick slices of
    French bread toasted
    Chicken-giblet *pâté*, or chicken-liver *pâté*
8 poached eggs
    Salt

Spread the toast lavishly and thickly with the *pâté* and place a poached egg on top. Serves 4.

TOASTED CHICKEN LIVER LOAF

A nice presentation.

1 loaf good bread or 1 loaf Pepperidge Farm
    (brown and serve) French bread
    Melted butter
2 tablespoons more butter
1 lb. chicken livers
1 tablespoon flour
½ cup heavy cream
1 jigger cognac, sherry or Madeira
    Salt, pepper

Slice the top off the loaf of bread neatly—whether it is the baked or the unbaked bread—and scoop out the inside with a sharp knife, making a neat box. Individual boxes may be made from 2-inch slices of hollowed-out French bread, though naturally without a lid. Brush inside and out with the melted butter and put in a 350° oven until a nice brown. Sauté the chicken livers in the 2 tablespoons of butter, sprinkle with the flour and add the heavy cream, liquor, salt and pepper. Cook until somewhat thickened, and then serve in the toasted loaf or individual boxes. Serves 4. Serve with hot rolls and a good tossed salad including quarters of tomatoes, hearts of artichoke and French dressing.

BAKED WILD RICE WITH GIBLETS

These, of course, are the giblets you have saved in the freezing unit from the various chickens you have cooked.

4 sets of giblets and necks
1 slice onion
1 slice lemon
1 teaspoon celery seed
  Salt, pepper
3 tablespoons butter
2 tablespoons flour
1 cup uncooked wild rice
1 teaspoon salt

Cook the giblets, except the livers, and the necks in 3 cups of water with the onion slice, lemon slice, celery seed and salt and pepper for about ½ hour or until tender. Remove from the liquid and chop the giblets into coarse dice, and remove the meat from the necks and cut up fine. Meanwhile, while the giblets were cooking, start the rice —well washed, of course—in a pan with 2 cups of water and 1 teaspoon salt. Bring to a boil, cover, turn the flame down and cook for about 40 minutes to 1 hour. Melt the butter and sauté the chicken livers briefly in it. Remove chicken livers from the pan, cut in small pieces and add to the other giblets. Add the flour to the butter in which the chicken livers were cooked and blend until smooth. Add salt, pepper and 2 cups of the strained liquid in which the giblets were cooked. Add the giblets to the gravy. Drain the rice if necessary, though all the liquid should be absorbed by this time. Place in a shallow baking dish and pour the giblet sauce or gravy on top. Bake in a 350° oven 20 to 30 minutes. Serves 4.

GIBLET AND RICE PIE

3 sets chicken giblets and necks
1 finely chopped onion
1 cup rice
3 tablespoons chicken fat, butter or
    bacon drippings
3 tablespoons flour
    Salt, pepper
1 teaspoon Worcestershire sauce
    Recipe for 1 pie crust, made according to
    basic recipe or from a ready-mix—or 2
    if you want a top crust

Simmer the giblets and the necks, except for the livers, with the onion, salt and pepper in 2 quarts of water until tender. Remove and dice the giblets, pull the meat from the necks and cut fine. Cook the rice in 2 cups of the broth from the giblets, bringing to a boil, covering and cooking over a very low flame for 14 minutes.

Meanwhile, make a gravy by melting the fat and blending in the flour. Add more salt and pepper to the gravy if necessary. Then add the Worcestershire sauce and 2 more cups of the chicken broth slowly, stirring until smooth and thickened. Add the chicken giblets, neck meat and livers which meanwhile have been sautéed in butter and diced. Line a pie tin with the dough and arrange the rice in the tin; then pour the giblets and gravy over the rice. Bake in a 450° oven 15 to 20 minutes or until brown. The top crust may or may not be used according to individual preference. Serves 4.

GIBLET GRAVY

Though a chicken neck isn't actually a giblet it is included always with the extra parts and should be used in gravy or in a broth. This gravy may be made to accompany a roast chicken, chicken cooked on a rotisserie, or a fried chicken; in fact, gravy and chicken cooked almost any way in which the giblets are left over fits in with the meal.

Chicken liver, heart, gizzard and neck
Salt, pepper
4 tablespoons butter or chicken fat
4 tablespoons flour
3 cups broth from the giblets

Rinse the liver, heart, gizzard (which has been carefully cleaned) and the neck. Put the gizzard, heart and neck in 3½ to 4 cups cold water with the salt and pepper and simmer for 15 to 20 minutes. Add the liver and cook 20 minutes longer or until all are tender. Remove the giblets, drain and chop fine. Remove the meat from the neck and cut it fine. Drain the broth and save. Heat the butter to a bubbling brown. Add the flour and stir until well cooked and blended. Strain and add the stock slowly. Cook until smooth and thickened. Add the chopped giblets. There should be 3 cups of stock; if there aren't, some milk or cream may be added or—more depressingly—water. This will make about 3 cups of gravy.

5

Fried—Deep Fat, Shallow, Whole or in Parts

BONELESS FRIED CHICKEN A LA CINTA

No salt, no pepper, no monosodium glutamate—just the good flavor of the chicken, which can be a surprise.

1 chicken (3 to 3½ lbs.)
Flour
3 eggs, beaten
Bread crumbs
¼ lb. butter
6 medium-sized mushrooms or 4 large ones
    that have been simmered with a little
    lemon juice
Grated Parmesan cheese
No salt
No pepper

Quarter the chicken, then bone each piece by slitting through the back with a knife. Leave a piece of the leg to give it shape. Pound the pieces thin like veal scallopini. Dust lightly with flour, dip in the eggs and then the bread crumbs. Pat the bread crumbs in by hand. Sauté slowly in the butter until they are a nice brown. Arrange on the broiler with the sautéed or boiled mushrooms on top, and sprinkle with the cheese. Put under a preheated broiler about 8 to 10 inches from the flame, if possible, until the cheese is bubbling and brown. Serves 4.

CHICKEN ALMANDINE

2 1½ to 2-lb. broilers, cut in quarters
3 tablespoons butter
⅔ cup blanched slivered almonds
1 cup white wine
   Salt, pepper
⅓ cup chopped parsley

Sauté the chicken and almonds in the butter until they are light brown on all sides. Add white wine, salt and pepper. Cover and cook over a very low flame for ½ hour or until tender. Add the parsley. Check the seasoning, adding more if necessary. Serve hot or cold. Serves 4.

CHICKEN AMBASSADOR

Chicken sautéed first, blazed with cognac and then simmered in that with some white wine.

1 chicken (about 2 to 2½ lbs.), cut in 4 parts
2 tablespoons butter
4 teaspoons cognac
½ cup white wine
1 shallot, chopped
1 small sprig parsley, chopped
   Salt, pepper

Sauté the chicken quickly in butter until all sides have a deep golden-brown color. Then pour 1 teaspoon of cognac on each quarter and set ablaze. (For easier flaming light the cognac in a separate pan and pour it onto the chicken while still alight.) Add the white wine, cover and cook slowly over a low fire until tender, about 30 minutes more. When nearly done add the shallot, parsley, salt and pepper. Serves 4.

CHICKEN SAUTÉED IN TARRAGON AND WHITE WINE

This is a recipe from Hubert Krenn, chef at Pierre's Restaurant in New York.

> 1 chicken (3 to 3½ lbs.), cut up as for frying
>   Flour
> 4 tablespoons butter
> 2 chopped shallots
> 1 tablespoon chopped fresh or 1 teaspoon dried
>   tarragon leaves, marinated in red-wine
>   vinegar
> ⅔ cup white wine
> 1 tablespoon more butter
> 1 teaspoon finely chopped onion
> 1 tablespoon flour
> ½ cup bouillon, with 1 tablespoon Italian
>   tomato paste if desired
>   Salt, pepper
> 1 tablespoon Worcestershire sauce,
>   sherry or Madeira

Dust the chicken lightly with flour and sauté in the butter until light brown. Add the shallots and cook over a low flame for a few minutes, then add the tarragon, white wine, salt, pepper and brown sauce made by cooking the onion slowly in 1 tablespoon of butter until light brown. Then blend in the flour and allow it to brown before stirring in the bouillon and tomato paste, salt, pepper, Worcestershire sauce, sherry or Madeira. Cover and cook slowly until chicken is done, which may be 45 to 50 minutes or more depending on the age and recent vigor of the chicken. Before serving cook the sauce a little longer if too thin. Serves 4.

CHICKEN CORN MEAL FRITTERS

In case you think this sounds quite a lot like a recipe for hush puppies, that's exactly what it is with raw chicken, cooked bacon and green pepper added. Serve, if you like, with a little mustard on the side.

> 1 cup corn meal (all Southerners use white, but actually either white or yellow will work)
> ½ cup sifted flour
> 2 teaspoons baking powder
> ½ teaspoon salt
> 1½ cups diced raw chicken (pull the frozen chicken breasts or legs off the bone and cut them up—it's that simple)
> 2 eggs, beaten
> ¾ cup milk
> 4 strips cooked crumbled bacon
> 1 small onion, chopped fine
> 1 thick slice green pepper, finely chopped

Mix the dry ingredients together, then add the chicken, then the beaten eggs and milk. Stir in the bacon, onion and green pepper. Drop by spoonful into deep fat heated to 375° and cook for about 8½ minutes or until the fritters are a crisp, golden brown. Drain on paper towels. Serves 4.

CHICKEN CUTLETS—NOT TO BE CONFUSED WITH CROQUETTES

These are of Russian derivation, and are very unlike those served at ladies' luncheons.

> 2 to 2½ cups uncooked chicken that has been ground twice
> 2 cups crumbled crustless French bread

½ cup heavy sweet cream
2 tablespoons vodka or gin
1 egg yolk
1 tablespoon flour
    Salt and paprika
¾ cup butter (1½ sticks)

Mix the chicken with the bread crumbs, sweet cream, vodka, egg yolk, flour, seasoning and 2 tablespoons of melted butter. Let stand in the refrigerator for ½ hour until the flavors have mingled. Shape into small oval cakes about 2 inches long and fry slowly on both sides in the rest of the butter until brown on both sides, about 20 minutes. Serves 4 when accompanied by fresh peas, tiny new potatoes cooked in their skins and served with parsley butter, a good green salad and hot fresh rolls.

CHICKEN IN RUM BATTER

When you get bored of all other ways of cooking chicken try this one.

½ cup sifted flour
½ cup Jamaica rum
1 tablespoon olive oil
2 egg whites, stiffly beaten
    Salt, pepper
1 chicken, 2 lbs., cut up as for frying
    Deep fat for frying

Mix the rum slowly into the flour so that it does not lump; add the olive oil, salt and pepper and then fold in the stiffly beaten egg whites. Dip the pieces of chicken into this batter and fry in deep fat heated to 350° for 12 to 13 minutes or until golden brown. Drain on paper towels. Serves 3 or 4.

CHICKEN AND CHEESE CROQUETTES

3 tablespoons butter
3 tablespoons flour
1 cup milk
2 cups diced cooked or canned chicken
⅓ cup grated Switzerland Swiss cheese
2 tablespoons poppy seeds
Salt, pepper
1 egg
Bread crumbs
Fat for deep frying

Melt the butter and add the flour, cooking over a low flame until well blended. Add the milk slowly, stirring until quite thick. Add the chicken, cheese, poppy seeds, salt and pepper. Chill in the refrigerator about 1 or 2 hours for easy handling. Roll into little balls about the size of a golf ball, dip in the egg and then in the bread crumbs and fry in deep fat, which has been heated to 375°, for 3 or 4 minutes. These may be served with peas and new potatoes for a light meal for 4, or made into balls about 1 inch in diameter and served with cocktails. How many they will serve depends, of course, on your guests and what kind of party it is.

CHICKEN AND LEMON RICE CROQUETTES

A slightly different and pleasing variation from the kind served at ladies' luncheons.

¾ cup diced cooked or canned chicken
1 cup cooked rice
1 teaspoon salt
Grated rind of 1 lemon

1 egg, beaten with 2 tablespoons lemon juice
Another egg, beaten
Cracker crumbs
Fat for deep frying (peanut oil seems best)

Mix the chicken, rice, salt, lemon rind and the egg beaten with the lemon juice, and chill together. Roll into balls— for some reason or other the traditional cone-shaped croquettes bore me to death. Dip in the other beaten egg and then into the crumbs, and deep fry in fat heated to 375° for 3 or 4 minutes or until brown. Drain on paper towels and serve sprinkled with finely chopped parsley. Serves 4.

CHICKEN FRIED IN CURRY BATTER

Still another version, and a rather spicy one at that, of the many, many ways of frying a chicken.

1 2½ to 3-lb. chicken, cut up for frying
Flour for dusting
Salt, pepper
1 cup flour
1 cup sour cream (the dairy kind)
¼ cup milk
More salt and pepper
2 tablespoons curry powder

Dust the pieces of chicken lightly with flour, and salt and pepper. Make a batter by mixing the 1 cup of flour and the sour cream, milk, salt, pepper and curry powder together. This should be rather thick. Dip each piece of the lightly floured chicken into this batter, and then put into a frying basket. Lower the basket into fat heated to 385° and cook for 10 to 12 minutes, turning occasionally, until brown all over. Naturally it is best to do a few pieces at a time except in a very large-size fryer. Serves 4.

CHICKEN MARYLAND

Traditionally this is batter-fried chicken served with corn fritters, salt pork or bacon and a cream gravy, but there are many legitimate and illegitimate variations of this dish and people sometimes become contentious about their preferences.

> 2 frying chickens (about 2 lbs. each), either quartered, halved or cut up for frying
> Cold milk
> Flour
> Salt, pepper
> 6 tablespoons fat, preferably butter or bacon drippings

Soak the chicken for about 1 hour in enough cold milk to keep moistened. This will make the meat juicy. Shake off surplus milk and put the pieces of chicken in a paper bag with flour, salt and pepper. Shake until the chicken is well coated. Sauté in the fat until brown on all sides. Cover the skillet, turn the heat down very, very low and cook until the chicken is tender, about 30 minutes, adding a little more fat if the pan starts to dry out. Serve with the creamy gravy and, to be authentic, with corn fritters and broiled bacon. Serves 4 to 6.

Cream gravy:

> 3 tablespoons fat from the pan
> 3 tablespoons flour
> 1 cup chicken broth or stock made from the giblets
> 1 cup cream
> Salt and pepper

Stir the chicken drippings with the flour, salt and pepper. Add the broth slowly, stirring until smooth and thick; then add the cream, stirring until that is smooth and thick. Add salt and pepper.

CHICKEN WITH WALNUT SAUCE

Here and there around the Mediterranean various people cook their chicken in a walnut sauce—and very good it is, and very simple to do!

> 1 chicken (about 2½ lbs.), cut up as for frying
> 2 tablespoons butter
> 1 small onion, chopped
>   Salt, flour, cayenne pepper, paprika
> 1½ cups milk
> 1 cup chopped walnuts (roughly, a 4-oz. can)
>   Simmer the giblets and neck in 1 cup water
>   with 1 slice lemon, 1 stalk celery, 1 slice
>   onion and seasoning

Sauté the pieces of chicken, except the giblets, in the butter until golden brown. Add the onion and cook with the chicken over a low flame until pale yellow. Sprinkle with the seasoning and add about ½ cup of the strained liquid from the giblets. Cover and simmer until tender. Blend the flour with enough of the cold milk to make a smooth paste, and then add the paste and the rest of the milk to the chicken. Cook for 5 or 10 minutes until the sauce is smooth. Sprinkle with the chopped walnuts and dot with a few more pieces of butter. Simmer for about 5 minutes more and serve with a colorful vegetable—peas or spinach or parsley potatoes. Serves 4.

CHICKEN SAUTÉ SEC

1 frying chicken (about 3½ lbs.), cut in
    pieces for serving
Flour
Salt, pepper
4 tablespoons butter
2 shallots or green onions, chopped fine
2 tablespoons chopped parsley
Sprinkling of thyme and basil
½ cup California sauterne or other white
    table wine
1 4-oz. can sliced mushrooms

Dust pieces of chicken with flour seasoned with salt and pepper. Melt butter in a large, heavy skillet. Sauté the chicken until golden brown, turning the pieces frequently and adding more butter if it starts to dry out. Add shallots, parsley, thyme, basil and wine. Cover and simmer gently for 30 minutes. Add the drained mushrooms. Cook for 15 or more minutes until the chicken is tender and the liquid has cooked away. Serves 3 or 4.

SALEM FRIED CHICKEN

1 chicken (about 2½ lbs.), cut up as for frying
⅛ teaspoon red pepper
¼ teaspoon black pepper
1 clove garlic, mashed or pressed
1 teaspoon ground ginger
½ teaspoon ground coriander seeds (optional)
    Salt
2 eggs, beaten lightly with 3 tablespoons water
    Bread crumbs or cracker crumbs
    Fat for deep frying

Remove skins from chicken pieces. Mix spices and mashed garlic, and rub thoroughly with fingers into each piece of chicken. Sprinkle lightly with salt. Place chicken in frying pan and add about ¼ cup of water or enough to cover bottom of pan. Cover tightly and simmer gently for about ½ hour or until tender. Remove cover last 10 minutes to cook juices in pan down to almost nothing. Roll each piece of chicken into fine crumbs. Dip 1 or 2 pieces at a time into egg mixture and then into the bread crumbs again. Drop immediately into deep hot fat and fry until golden brown, about 1 to 2 minutes. Drain on paper towels and keep in warm place. Continue frying until all the chicken is done. Serve immediately. Serves 3 or 4.

CHICKEN IN THE BASKET

Chicken in the Basket is easy to serve and it is legal to use your fingers. Serve it, a half chicken to a person, in a napkin-lined breadbasket.

> 2 packages of quick-frozen frying chickens
> ½ cup flour
> 1 teaspoon salt
> Pepper
> 3 or 4 tablespoons fat for frying

Defrost chicken pieces and shake in a paper bag with the flour and seasonings until lightly coated. Melt the fat in a heavy skillet and brown chicken. Cook over low heat about 45 minutes longer or until the chicken is tender. Drain on paper towels before putting in the baskets. Serve with a tossed green salad, hot rolls and French-fried potatoes. Serves 4.

DEEP FRIED CHICKEN PÂTÉ PIES

Actually these are made with biscuits rather than pie dough, but that's the general idea. These make a rather robust but impressive morsel to serve with cocktails—impressive, at least, out of all proportion to the amount of work—or they can be served for a meal.

> ½ lb. fresh or frozen chicken livers
> 4 tablespoons sweet butter
> ½ jigger brandy
> Salt, pepper
> 1 package buttermilk biscuits in a tube
> Deep fat for frying

Sauté the chicken livers in butter until barely tender. Either chop fine and add salt, pepper and brandy; or, better yet, let cool slightly and put in an electric blender with the brandy and salt and pepper for 30 to 40 seconds. Pull the biscuits apart and put a spoonful of this mixture on each biscuit; then fold biscuits over and pinch together. Deep fry for slightly more than 1 minute or until brown and crunchy in fat heated to 375°. Drain on paper towels. Serve hot or cold as you wish—naturally the hot is a little better. With these proportions there will be some chicken-liver *pâté* left to spread on hot toast for another day. Makes enough pies for 4 people for a meal.

CHICKEN SAUTÉED WITH FRESH MUSHROOMS

> 4 tablespoons butter
> ½ lb. mushrooms, sliced lengthwise through
> the caps and stems
> 1 chicken (2½ to 3 lbs.), cut up as for frying

⅓ cup finely chopped parsley
Juice of 1 lemon
Salt, pepper

Sauté the mushrooms in the butter, remove them from the pan and save them. Sauté slowly the pieces of chicken until tender and golden brown on all sides. When done add the mushrooms, parsley, lemon juice, salt and pepper. Warm together for 1 or 2 minutes and serve. Serves 4.

FRIED CHICKEN WITH PARSLEY GRAVY

There is literally no end to the ways of frying chicken and to the sauces that go with it. This one is a semideep-fried chicken.

1 chicken (2½ to 3 lbs.), cut up as for frying
Flour, salt and pepper
1 cup lard
2 cups milk
⅓ cup finely chopped parsley

Shake the pieces of chicken in a paper bag with flour, salt and pepper until very lightly coated. Heat the lard in a heavy skillet and brown the chicken on both sides. Turn the heat down, cover the skillet and cook until the chicken is tender and done, which will be about 15 minutes. Remove the chicken from the skillet and drain on paper towels. Pour off all the fat, except about 2 tablespoons. Add 2 tablespoons flour. Stir until well blended. Add salt and pepper, and then the milk very slowly. Cook until smooth and thick, but not real thick. Add parsley. Add the pieces of chicken and cook until chicken is tender and the sauce is slightly reduced, about 10 to 15 minutes more. Serves 4.

WHOLE FRIED CHICKEN, CHINESE FASHION

Yes, it is a trick, but guaranteed to amuse your guests. Besides, it's an old Chinese custom.

> 1 whole chicken (2½ to 3 lbs.)
> Flour
> Salt and pepper
> Fat for deep frying

Remove the giblets and save those for another day, another recipe. Lightly flour and season the chicken inside and out. Heat fat for deep frying, preferably peanut oil, to 400°. Drop the whole chicken into the fat and cook for about 35 minutes or until the thigh pierced with a fork shows no pink. That's all. Obviously, without intending to be a commercial, this will only fit into the Presto Dixie fryer basket or a nonelectric one improvised at home. In the current models of the others the baskets are not quite large enough, though this is not meant as any criticism of those fryers. Serves 4.

NORMANDY CHICKEN

With a chicken, some cream, mushrooms and cognac as a start the French can go on cooking quite happily and indefinitely, varying slightly the proportions and the additional minor ingredients. This is one of their more amiable variations.

> 1 chicken (about 2 to 2½ lbs.), cut up as
>   for frying
> ½ lb. mushrooms, sliced thin
> 1½ tablespoons butter
> 2 tablespoons cognac
> ¼ cup heavy sweet cream
> Juice of 1 lemon

Sauté the chicken in the butter with the mushrooms until the pieces of chicken are golden brown. Add the cognac, cream and lemon juice and let simmer over a hot flame until the chicken is tender, about 25 to 30 minutes. Serve piping hot. Serves 4.

CURRIED CHICKEN SAUTÉ

1 chicken (about 3½ lbs.), cut up as for frying
    Salt and pepper
2 tablespoons butter
2 tablespoons olive oil
1 tablespoon minced onion
1 cup California Rhine wine, sauterne or
    other white table wine
5 tablespoons flour
2 teaspoons good strong curry powder
1 cup heavy cream or undiluted evaporated
    milk
2 tablespoons finely chopped parsley
    Salt

Dust pieces of chicken with salt and pepper. Heat the butter and oil in a large, heavy skillet with a tight-fitting lid. Add chicken and sauté to a golden brown, turning the pieces frequently. Sprinkle onion over the chicken. Add wine and ½ cup water. Cover tightly and simmer gently for 45 minutes to 1 hour or until chicken is tender. Remove chicken to a serving platter and keep warm. Mix flour and curry powder to a smooth paste with a little of the cream, and add to liquid in skillet. Add remaining cream and cook, stirring constantly, until the mixture is thick and smooth. Add parsley and salt to taste. Pour gravy over chicken or serve separately. Serve with hot, cooked rice. Serves 4.

FRIED CHICKEN WITH GRAVY

A less fattening version of the very fattening Chicken and Gravy.

> 3 lbs. chicken, cut in pieces for frying
> Salt
> Pepper
> Flour
> Shortening
> 5 tablespoons drippings
> 4 tablespoons flour
> 6 tablespoons nonfat dry milk
> 1 teaspoon salt
> ½ teaspoon paprika, if desired
> ⅛ teaspoon pepper

Sprinkle pieces of chicken with salt and pepper. Dredge heavily with flour. Fry chicken in 2 inches of hot fat in skillet. Brown well on both sides. Lower heat and cover tightly with lid. Cook slowly, turning pieces occasionally, until chicken is tender. Remove chicken to hot platter and keep warm while making gravy.

Gravy:

Remove all but 5 tablespoons of drippings from pan. Combine flour, nonfat dry milk powder, salt, paprika and pepper. Add to drippings in pan, stirring until well blended. Gradually stir in 2 cups of water. Cook over low heat, stirring constantly, until thickened and smooth. Serve hot around chicken or serve separately in gravy boat. Serves 4.

ITALIAN FRIED CHICKEN

Many Southerners are good cooks, as are Northerners, Easterners, Westerners and all other regionalists, but they are their own very best publicity agents. Sure, their fried chicken is good as served in their homes but seldom in their restaurants, and others fry chicken well, too.

> 1 chicken (about 2½ lbs.), cut up for frying
> Flour
> 2 tablespoons lemon juice
> ¼ cup olive oil
> 1 bay leaf
> Salt, fresh-ground black pepper
> ⅓ cup fresh-grated Parmesan cheese (it's work, but that tired grocery-store stuff is pretty flavorless)
> ½ cup butter

Pick over the chicken, and flour it very lightly by shaking a few pieces at a time in a paper bag with about ⅓ cup of flour in it. Then lay the pieces of chicken in a marinade made by mixing the lemon juice, olive oil, bay leaf and a suitable amount of salt and pepper together. Let them stay in this at least 1 hour, turning the pieces from time to time so that all are well moistened.

Remove from the marinade and roll the moist but not dripping pieces in the grated cheese. Sauté in butter over a low heat until golden and tender. This must be done slowly or it will burn. Serves 4.

FRIED COOKED CHICKEN SERVED WITH HOT TOMATO GRAVY

1 boiled fowl, cut into serving pieces
2 tablespoons lemon juice
½ teaspoon mixed pickling spices
4 tablespoons olive oil
Salt, pepper
Beaten egg yolk
Bread crumbs
Fat for deep frying

Marinate the cooked chicken in the lemon juice, spices, olive oil and pepper for several hours. Shake off surplus liquid, dip in the egg yolk, which has been beaten with 2 tablespoons of water, and then dip into the bread crumbs. Fry in deep fat heated to 375° for 4 to 5 minutes or until golden brown. Drain on paper towels and serve with the following tomato gravy.

Tomato gravy:

5 tablespoons bacon drippings or butter
1 small onion, finely chopped
5 tablespoons flour
3 cups chicken broth
3 tablespoons Italian tomato paste
Salt and pepper

Cook the onion in the bacon drippings, add the flour and cook for a few minutes, then slowly add the broth and the tomato paste. Cook until thickened. Check the seasoning, add salt and pepper, if necessary, and serve hot with the fried chicken. Serves 4 to 6, depending on the size of the boiled chicken.

NASSI GORENG

An Indonesian mish-mash of bits of this and that, combined with curried fried rice.

⅓ cup butter
2 tablespoons curry powder
1 cup uncooked rice
Salt, pepper
2 cups chicken broth
4 to 6 green onions, tops and bottoms chopped
1 buffet-size-can shrimp, cleaned
1 cup diced cooked or canned chicken

Add the curry powder to the melted butter and stir until smooth. Add the rice and stir around until all the rice is coated with the spicy butter. Add salt, pepper, onion tops and bottoms, and chicken broth. Bring to a boil and cover; turn heat down low and cook for 14 minutes. Add shrimp and chicken and reheat until they are hot. To be authentic top each serving with lengthwise strips of cucumber and/or poached egg. Serves 4.

COTELETTE KIEV

A classic Russian recipe as implausible-sounding as baked Alaska, but tasting, I think, much, much better and well worth the slight bother of preparing. I'm not sure but what I think it one of the very best of all chicken recipes.

> 3 whole breasts of chicken or 6 fresh or
>   frozen halves
> ½ lb. sweet butter
> 2 eggs, beaten
>   Bread crumbs, very fine
>   Salt and pepper
>   Fat or oil for deep-fat frying

Remove the bone from the breasts of chicken. Cut the breast in two, and pound flat and very thin. Cut off the gristle. One half breast makes a portion.

The butter is shaped into an egg-shaped roll about 3 inches long and about 1 inch wide at its thickest point, and chilled in this shape before using. Place the butter roll in the breast, roll the chicken around it and fold the flaps in, completely encasing the butter.

Roll the cotelette in the beaten eggs, then in the bread crumbs. Repeat the whole procedure until each piece is rolled in butter and crumbs. Fry in vegetable shortening or oil until brown, making certain that the oil isn't too hot; then bake in a hot oven for 8 or 10 minutes. Serves 6.

Caution: If the butter roll isn't completely tucked in, all your work will be in vain because it will leak out as it melts.

FRIED CHICKEN, SLIGHTLY DIFFERENT

    2 2½ to 3-lb. chickens, cut up
    1 tablespoon salt
    ¼ teaspoon pepper
    ¼ teaspoon monosodium glutamate
    1 small onion
    8 whole cloves
    1 egg
    1 cup milk
    1 cup flour
    1 teaspoon salt
    ¼ teaspoon pepper
    1 teaspoon paprika
      Fat for frying

Put cut-up chicken, salt, pepper, monosodium glutamate, onion and cloves in a pressure cooker with 1 cup of water, and cook under pressure for 5 minutes. Or cook chicken in open kettle until barely tender, 35 to 40 minutes. Drain and cool. Then dip pieces into a mixture made of the beaten egg and milk. Make sure the pieces are well coated. Into a paper bag put the flour, salt, pepper and paprika and shake well. Then add the egg-milk-dipped chicken pieces to the mixture in the paper bag and shake. Then dip pieces into egg-milk mixture again, then back into bag for a second coating of seasoned flour. Heat fat (any you choose) about ½ inch deep in 2 frying pans and cook chicken slowly until golden brown. Serves 6 to 8.

⑥

Miscellaneous

BAKED CHICKEN PUFF

Prepare 4 chicken-and-cheese sandwiches using 8 slices of buttered *good* bread, thin slices of cooked chicken and thin slices of Cheddar or rattrap cheese. Arrange sandwiches in a greased, shallow baking pan. Mix together:

> 3 eggs, slightly beaten
> 1½ cups milk
> ½ cup California sherry wine
> Salt, celery salt and pepper to taste

Pour mixture over sandwiches and let stand for 1 hour or so. Bake in a slow oven, 325°, for 1 hour. To serve, separate sandwiches with a sharp knife and lift onto plates with a broad spatula. Accompany with a green salad. Serves 4.

CHICKEN MORE OR LESS EN PAPILLOTE

This is a good party dish because it is simple to prepare ahead of time and the tidy aluminum packages, 1 to a customer, are decorative and very pretty and the exact cooking time doesn't seem to matter at all.

1 chicken (2½ to 3 lbs.), cut in quarters
1½ cups shortening, preferably butter
12 small white onions
12 even pretty mushroom caps
    Salt, pepper
1 tablespoon chopped parsley
½ cup light cream
    Aluminum foil

Brown the chicken quarters lightly in the fat. Remove and drain on paper towels. Brown the onion and mushrooms very briefly in the same fat. Tear off 4 pieces of aluminum foil a little larger than 1 foot square. Place on each piece of foil 1 quarter of a chicken, 3 of the onions and 3 of the mushroom caps. Salt and pepper lightly and sprinkle with ¼ of the parsley and 2 tablespoons of cream. Bring the edges of the foil up, carefully fold over lengthwise and then roll up the ends good and tight. Place the packages on a cooky sheet and bake in a 400° oven for 1 hour or longer. It doesn't make any difference if, for any reason, the party is delayed somewhat. Double or triple the recipe if desired. When prepared ahead of time be sure to take the packages out of the refrigerator an hour or two before baking to allow them to come to room temperature. To serve, put 1 to each plate, cut crosses in the aluminum foil and fold corners back decoratively. This amount serves 4.

CHICKEN AND ALMOND RING

Delicate, savory and comparatively nonfattening.

1¾ cups dry bread crumbs
½ cup nonfat dry milk
2 bouillon cubes
2 cups chopped chicken
1 egg
1 teaspoon rubbed sage
½ teaspoon black pepper
3 tablespoons grated onion
¼ cup finely chopped almonds

Combine bread crumbs and nonfat dry milk powder in a bowl; blend well. Dissolve bouillon cubes in 2 cups of hot water. Add to bread-crumb mixture and mix thoroughly. Add chicken and mix well. Stir in egg, sage, pepper, onion and almonds. Spoon into buttered 8-inch ring mold and bake in moderate oven, 350°, for 30 minutes. Serve with mushroom sauce. Serves 6.

Mushroom sauce:

1½ cups water
⅓ cup nonfat dry milk
3 tablespoons flour
½ teaspoon salt
½ teaspoon rubbed sage
Dash of black pepper
1 3-oz. can sliced mushrooms

Pour water into top of double boiler. Combine dry milk powder, flour, salt, sage and pepper. Sprinkle over surface of water. Beat with rotary beater just until blended. Place over boiling water and cook, stirring constantly until thickened, about 5 to 8 minutes. Stir in sliced mushrooms. Serve hot over Chicken and Almond Ring.

CHICKEN COOKED IN A MUSHROOM AND WINE SAUCE

From the chef at the hotel in Dormans, on the way to Paris from Rheims, comes this style of cooking chicken, which is plain heavenly and yet does not require a too involved technique. Sometimes, adding the egg yolks is slightly complicated, so if it makes you nervous leave them out; the sauce will be a little thinner but will have the same good flavor.

> 1 chicken (about 2½ lbs.), cut in quarters
> ½ stick butter (¼ cup)
> 1 jigger cognac
> 1 cup dry white wine
> Salt, pepper
> 1 cup heavy cream
> ¼ lb. mushrooms, just the small caps (use the stems for something else)
> 1 tablespoon butter
> 2 egg yolks

Sauté the quarters of chicken in butter until brown all over. Pour the brandy over the chicken and light it. When the flame goes out add the white wine and seasoning; cover and simmer until tender. Meanwhile, cook the mushrooms gently and briefly in the tablespoon of butter and add to the chicken with the cream, reserving 2 tablespoons of the cream. Just before serving check the seasoning, remove from the stove and add the egg yolks that have been beaten in the 2 tablespoons of saved cream. Do not cook any farther. Serves 4 glamorously.

BAKED IDAHO POTATOES WITH CHICKEN AND CRAB MEAT SAUCE

Delicate yet robust food.

> 4 large handsome potatoes, matching in size
> 4 tablespoons butter
> 2 cups (1 pint) sour cream
> 1 tablespoon tarragon vinegar and a sprig of tarragon chopped, if available, either fresh or in vinegar
> 1 can (6 ozs.) boned chicken, diced
> 1 can (6 ozs.) crab meat or lobster, well picked over

Scrub the potatoes thoroughly and butter the skins lightly. Bake in a 350° oven until tender when pricked with a fork. This will be at least 1 hour, depending on how large the potatoes are. Meanwhile, put in a pan the sour cream, tarragon vinegar, chicken and crab meat that has been picked over to remove the thin membranes. When the potatoes are done slash with a cross to let the steam escape and, with your fingers protected by a towel, carefully push each potato in the middle to fluff up. Put a lump of the butter in each and pour the chicken-and-crab-meat sauce that has been warmed, but not cooked, over each of the opened fluffed potatoes. Serves 4.

CHICKEN ALMOND

A Chinese dish, American fashion.

> 2 cups cubed cooked chicken
> 2 tablespoons butter
> ½ cup crushed pineapple

½ cup pineapple juice
1½ tablespoons cornstarch
2 cups chicken stock
½ cup slivered toasted almonds
½ cup sliced celery
1½ teaspoons salt

Sauté the pineapple in butter for 5 minutes. Add pineapple juice mixed with cornstarch. Add chicken stock
and stir over low heat until thickened. Add cubed chicken,
almonds, celery and salt. Let heat through. Serve with
chow-mein noodles. Serves 6 to 8.

CHICKEN AND CORN BREAD SHORTCAKE,
AS IT WERE

This is very streamlined—good for those who work and
cook too.

1 batch corn bread, made from a good ready-
    mix according to directions on box and
    baked in muffin form if desired
Butter
2 cups diced cooked or canned chicken
1 can undiluted condensed cream-of-mushroom
    soup
3 strips cooked crumbled bacon
Salt, pepper

Split the squares or muffins of hot corn bread and butter
them. Between the halves and on top place the chicken,
which has been heated with the mushroom soup, and the
bacon. The salt and pepper should be added judiciously—
the soup has lots. Serves 4.

BAKED TOMATOES WITH CHICKEN FILLING

8 firm handsome tomatoes, all nearly the
    same size
2 tablespoons butter
2 tablespoons flour
1 cup chicken broth
    Salt, pepper
2 cups finely diced cooked or canned chicken
½ cup bread crumbs
⅓ cup finely chopped parsley
2 tablespoons butter

Slice off the top of the tomatoes, scoop out the center part
and turn upside down to drain while you mix the filling.
Melt the first lot of butter and stir in the flour. Add the
chicken broth slowly, stirring until smooth and thickened.
Season with salt and pepper and add the diced chicken.
Divide into 8 parts and fill the tomatoes, packing in fairly
firmly. Sprinkle the tops with the bread crumbs mixed
with the parsley, and dot with the second lot of butter.
Bake 15 to 20 minutes in a 350° oven, spooning some of
the juices that will be in the bottom of the pan over the
top of the bread crumbs. Serves 4.

CHICKEN AND ALMOND SPREAD

A fancy filling for tea sandwiches.

1 cup cooked or canned chicken, put through
    meat grinder with the coarse blade
1 cup blanched shelled almonds, also put
    through the meat grinder with the coarse
    blade
¼ cup heavy cream, whipped until stiff

1 tablespoon sherry
Salt, pepper

Mix the ground chicken and almonds together; add the sherry, salt and pepper and then the whipped cream, folding in gently. Spread thinly on thin bread-and-butter sandwiches to serve with fine tea. Makes a little more than 2 cups.

CHICKEN BREASTS ON SAUTÉED EGGPLANT WITH SOUBISE SAUCE

8 chicken breasts
8 slices eggplant
Milk
Seasoned flour
2 tablespoons butter
1 large onion, chopped very fine
⅓ cup sweet butter
3 tablespoons flour
1½ cups chicken bouillon
½ cup finely chopped parsley
Salt, pepper

Lightly butter and season the chicken breasts and roast in the oven heated to 350° until tender. Meanwhile, dip the slices of eggplant in the milk and then in flour and sauté in the butter until tender and brown on both sides. Drain and keep warm. Make the sauce by sautéing the onion in the butter until pale yellow and soft. Stir in the flour and cook until thickened and smooth; then add the bouillon slowly, stirring constantly, until somewhat thickened. Add salt, pepper and parsley. Arrange 1 chicken breast on each slice of eggplant and pour the soubise sauce over all. Serves 4.

CHICKEN AND ALMOND CUSTARD

2 cups diced cooked or canned chicken
1 pint milk, scalded
2 eggs, beaten
½ teaspoon dried tarragon
    Salt, pepper
3 strips crumbled cooked bacon
¼ cup blanched slivered toasted almonds

Arrange the chicken, bacon and almonds in custard cups or baking dishes. Pour the scalded milk slowly over the beaten eggs; blend, add seasoning, then pour over the chicken. Set the dishes in a pan of hot water in a 350° oven for 1 hour or more. The custard is done when a knife inserted in the sides comes out clean. Or better yet, cook it, 4 custard cups at a time, on a rack in a pressure cooker with ½ cup water. Carefully cover each of the cups with wax paper and tie it on firmly. Bring up to 15 lbs. pressure, cook for 2 minutes and reduce pressure gradually. Pressure-cooked custards have a specially delicate texture—the only drawback is the top doesn't have any pretty brown. Makes about 6 custard cups.

CHICKEN CUSTARD

Served cold in brown custard cups on a very hot day, this is an extremely pleasant way of beginning a light summer meal.

1 cup heavy cream
1 cup chicken broth, preferably strong
    homemade
3 egg yolks, beaten
1 tablespoon sherry
    Salt

Scald the cream in chicken broth; let cool slightly before pouring over the beaten egg yolks. Add sherry and salt and pour into custard cups; place in a pan of hot water in a 325° oven for 1 hour or more, or until a clean knife inserted at the edges comes out clean. Chill before serving. These may be cooked on a rack in a pressure pan also. Cover each cup with wax paper and securely tie a string around it (elastic bands give way). Add 1 cup water, bring up to 15 lbs. pressure for 2 minutes and reduce pressure gradually. Serves 4 to 5, depending on the size of your custard cups.

CHICKEN AND CLAM SOUFFLÉ

3 tablespoons butter
3 tablespoons flour
1 can minced clams (7 ozs.), drain but
   save the liquid
1 cup juice from the clams, or juice from the
   clams plus enough milk to complete the cup
Salt, pepper
1 can boned chicken (8 ozs.), chopped fine
⅓ cup finely chopped parsley
3 eggs, separated

Melt the butter, blend in the flour and add the liquid, salt and pepper, stirring constantly until smooth and thick. Stir in the minced clams and chopped chicken. Remove from the fire, blend in the egg yolks and fold in the stiffly beaten whites and the parsley. Turn into a greased baking dish with straight sides and bake in a 350° oven for about 45 to 50 minutes or until the top is golden brown and springs back when lightly touched. Serve with a colorful salad and bacon biscuits made by adding crumbled cooked bacon to drop-biscuit mix. Serves 4.

CHICKEN CAKES WITH CURRY SAUCE

A pleasing and slightly different way of serving a chicken curry. The dry skim milk gives the chicken a good flavor and some substance, but is easy on the figure and the food bills.

> 1 cup dry bread crumbs
> ½ teaspoon celery salt
> ¼ teaspoon powdered thyme
> ⅛ teaspoon black pepper
> ⅔ cup nonfat dry milk
> 2 chicken bouillon cubes
> 2 eggs
> 2 cups finely chopped cooked chicken

Put bread crumbs, celery salt, thyme, pepper and nonfat dry milk powder in a bowl, and mix together. Dissolve bouillon cubes in 1 cup of water. Pour over crumbs and blend well. Beat in eggs, add chicken and mix. Turn into 6 3-inch greased cups of muffin pan. Bake in a moderate oven, 350°, until tops are firm and golden brown, about 15 minutes. Serve hot with curry sauce and rice. Serves 6.

Curry sauce:

> 6 tablespoons nonfat dry milk
> 4 tablespoons flour
> 1 teaspoon salt
> 1 to 2 teaspoons curry powder
> ⅛ teaspoon black pepper
> 2 tablespoons butter
> ½ cup raisins, plumped briefly in boiling
>   water, then drained

Pour 2 cups water into top of double boiler. Sprinkle nonfat dry milk powder, flour, salt, curry powder and pepper over top of water. Beat with rotary beater until just blended. Add butter and cook over gently boiling water, stirring constantly, until thickened. Stir in raisins. Serve hot over Chicken Cakes.

CHICKEN PAPRIKA

This is a classic Hungarian version which fits well into our ways of cooking and eating.

> 2 2½-lb. broiler-size chickens, cut at the joints
> 4 tablespoons finely chopped onion sautéed in
> ½ tablespoon butter until light gold
> 1 tablespoon Hungarian paprika
> 1 cup chicken stock
> 1 green pepper, chopped
> 1 tomato, chopped fine
> 1 clove garlic, chopped fine
> 2 teaspoons salt
> 1 cup sour cream
> ½ cup heavy cream
> 2 teaspoons flour

Simmer the butter and partly cooked onions with the chicken stock, green pepper, tomato, garlic and salt for 10 minutes. Add the pieces of chicken and cover. Simmer for 25 minutes. Add the sour cream, the heavy cream and ¼ cup cold water. Add the flour and mix until smooth. Remove the chicken and cook the sauce for 5 minutes more.

Serve with *spaetzle* made this way: Take 3 eggs and 4½ tablespoons of flour and a pinch of salt. Mix into a smooth dough. Put on a small wet breadboard. Take a wet knife and cut into inch-wide strips with the dull side of the knife. Cut these strips in 1-inch pieces into a pan of boiling water. They are done when they come to the top. Drain and sauté in butter. Serves 6.

CHICKEN PIROSHKI

Make a plain pie dough by blending gently and briefly 2½ cups sifted all-purpose flour, 1 teaspoon salt, ¾ cup short-ening, preferably cold lard, and 5 to 6 tablespoons cold water. Roll out and cut in 12 to 14 (4½ to 5-inch) circles.

Filling:

> 2 tablespoons chopped onion
> ¼ cup butter
> 2 tablespoons flour
> ½ cup California Burgundy or claret
> ½ cup chicken stock (canned or bouillon-cube
>   chicken broth may be used)
> 2 tablespoons chopped parsley
> ½ teaspoon Worcestershire sauce
> ½ teaspoon poultry seasoning
>   Salt and pepper to taste
> 2 cups ground cooked chicken (giblets too)
> 2 hard-cooked eggs, chopped
>   Milk or egg white (nice but not necessary)

Sauté onion gently in butter for 5 minutes. Blend in flour.

Add wine and stock. Cook, stirring constantly, until mixture boils and thickens. Remove from heat. Add all remaining ingredients, mixing well.

Heap some of this mixture in the center of each circle of dough. Moisten edges of dough with cold water, fold over to form semicircles and pinch together on the ends. Place on a baking sheet. Press edges of pastry together with a fork and prick tops. Brush tops with unbeaten egg white or milk. Bake in a hot oven, 450°, for 15 to 20 minutes or until delicately browned. Serve hot. Makes 12 to 14 piroshki.

Serve with a vegetable and a salad for dinner, or as a delicious main dish with a mushroom sauce for a buffet supper. Tiny piroshki make extra special hot hors d'oeuvres.

CHICKEN CLUB SANDWICH

Substantial but not too original provender for those sudden unscheduled hungers that come up every now and then.

> 3 slices toasted buttered good white bread
> Sliced cooked chicken
> Lettuce
> Mayonnaise
> 3 slices cooked crumbled bacon
> 2 slices tomato

Cover 1 slice of buttered toast with the chicken, lettuce and mayonnaise. Then on the second slice of toast put another piece of lettuce and the slices of tomato. Spread with mayonnaise, sprinkle with the bacon and top with a third slice of toast. This makes 1 sandwich, but cut it into quarters and secure with toothpicks for easier eating.

CHICKEN BREASTS SOMEWHAT BENEDICT

This is taking liberties, justifiable however, I think, with a fine old recipe.

> 8 chicken breasts
> 3 tablespoons butter
> 4 English muffins, split and toasted
> 8 slices cooked ham
>> Hollandaise sauce, made according to a basic recipe or bought ready-made, or even a cheese sauce

Roast the chicken breasts, basting with butter, 45 to 50 minutes or until tender. Arrange the muffins with a slice of ham on each and a chicken breast on that and cover with the hollandaise sauce. Serves 4 for Sunday breakfast or lunch.

CHICKEN IN CRANBERRY SAUCE ON WATER CRESS BISCUITS

> 2 cups diced cooked or canned chicken
> Salt, pepper
> 1-lb. can cranberry sauce
> 1 buffet-size can small boiled onions, partially drained
> 1 batch drop biscuits, made from any ready-mix but with ⅓ cup chopped water cress added
> Butter

Mix the chicken, cranberry and onions in a saucepan with a little but not all of the juice of the onions, and heat until it becomes a nice fragrant sauce. Split the hot water-cress biscuits, butter them and put some of the chicken and cranberry sauce between them and some on top of them. Serves 4.

CHICKEN IN CURRY CREAM WITH ASPARAGUS TIPS

> 1 chicken (2½ to 3 lbs.), cut up as for
> frying
> 4 tablespoons butter
> 1 cup bouillon
> 1 jigger port wine—the white port looks pret-
> tier but most people do not have that
> around—or Madeira or sherry
> Salt, cayenne
> 1½ tablespoons good curry powder
> 2 tablespoons flour
> 1 cup heavy cream
> 1 lb. fresh or 1 box frozen asparagus, which will
> be approximately the same in usable weight
> More salt

Sauté the chicken in the butter until a golden brown on all sides. Add the bouillon and port or other wine with the salt, cayenne and curry powder. Cover and simmer until tender. Meanwhile, cook the asparagus in boiling salted water until tender. Drain and keep warm. Mix the flour to a thin paste with the cream, gradually adding all the cream. Add to the chicken and cook a few minutes more until it is well blended. Arrange the hot asparagus on a platter and the chicken in the curry-cream sauce on top. Serves 4.

CHICKEN PRESSURE COOKED AND THEN ROASTED WITH PECANS

1 chicken (about 2½ to 3 lbs.), cut in quarters
1 lemon
  Salt, pepper
2 tablespoons butter
1 tablespoon finely chopped parsley
1 tablespoon finely chopped chives
¼ teaspoon, which is to say a mere smidgeon,
  of rosemary
  Salt
½ teaspoon powdered sugar
3 crusts stale bread, grated
¼ cup coarsely chopped pecans

Rub chicken quarters with cut lemon on both sides, and salt and pepper generously. Cook in pressure cooker with ½ cup of water 10 minutes at 10 lbs. pressure after it has been brought up to pressure. Reduce pressure immediately. Meanwhile, melt butter and add parsley, chives, rosemary, salt and sugar. Mix the grated bread crusts with the nuts. Dip the pieces of chicken in the butter mixture and then in the bread-crumb-and-nut mixture. Arrange on a broiler and place rack about 3 or 4 inches from the heat. Broil on one side for 5 minutes then turn and broil on the other side 5 minutes longer. Serves 4.

CHICKEN, TOMATO AND GREEN OLIVE SOUFFLÉ

1 cup cooked or canned chicken, finely chopped
3 tablespoons Italian tomato paste
⅓ cup finely sliced pimiento-stuffed olives
3 tablespoons butter

3 tablespoons flour
1 cup chicken broth
   Salt, pepper
1 teaspoon dried basil or 1 tablespoon finely
   chopped fresh basil
3 eggs, separated

Melt the butter, blend in the flour and add the chicken broth slowly, stirring until smooth and quite thick. Blend in the tomato paste thoroughly. Remove from the stove and stir in the egg yolks, chicken and olives. Fold in the stiffly beaten egg whites and turn into a buttered baking dish, preferably with straight sides. Place in a 350° oven for 50 minutes or until the top is brown and springs back when lightly touched. Serves 4.

CHICKEN TURNOVERS

Simple, basic, but not routine.

Pastry dough for 2-crust pie
2 cups diced cooked chicken
3 tablespoons butter
¼ cup chopped onion
¼ cup chopped green pepper
3 tablespoons flour
1½ cups milk or stock

Melt fat, add onions and green pepper and cook until translucent. Blend in flour and add liquid, stirring constantly until thick. To ½ of the sauce add the cubed chicken. Save the remaining sauce to heat and pour over baked turnovers. Cut pastry into 4-inch circles. Put 2 circles together with 1 tablespoonful of chicken filling between. Crimp edges and bake at 450° for 25 to 30 minutes. Serves 4 to 6.

CHICKEN WITH SHRIMP

This is a shockingly free adaption of one of Ali Bab's, which he probably would not even recognize.

    ½ lb. mushrooms, sliced
     3 tablespoons butter
     1 small onion, chopped fine
     1 teaspoon finely chopped parsley
    ½ cup white wine
     2 dozen shrimp, peeled and deveined
     2 tablespoons cognac
     2 tablespoons butter
     1 whole chicken (about 2½ lbs.)
      Egg yolk
      Grated bread crumbs
     1 tablespoon flour
      Juice of 1 lemon
    ½ teaspoon thyme
     1 bay leaf
      Salt, pepper, paprika

Cook the mushrooms in the butter, add the onion and cook until pale yellow then add the parsley and white wine and simmer. In the meantime, pan-roast the pieces of chicken sprinkled with salt and pepper in a 325° oven for about 1 hour, basting occasionally with butter. Cook the shrimp in 2 tablespoons of butter over a low flame 3 to 5 minutes or until barely pink. Set aside. Put the pieces of chicken in a casserole and add the shrimp and the butter in which they cooked. Pour in the cognac and light. Meanwhile, add the rest of the ingredients to the mushroom-and-white-wine concoction. Pour over the chicken and shrimp, and heat together briefly just time enough for the flavors to get barely acquainted. Serves 4.

CHICKEN PHILPY

This is an honest old Southern bread in an unorthodox
version. The original does not include the chicken and
green pepper. This does, however, make a nice improvised
meal with a green salad on the side. Both this and the original are baked in a pie tin, cut into wedges and split and
buttered while hot. This makes a good picnic dish when
served unheated, or kept hot in a bag insulated with
Fiberglas.

> ½ cup corn meal
> ½ cup milk
> 1 cup cooked rice
> 2 eggs
> 2 tablespoons melted butter
> 3 slices bacon, cut in pieces
> 1 cup diced cooked or canned chicken
> ½ medium-size green pepper, chopped and
>   seeds removed
> Salt
> Pepper

Scald the corn meal in the milk and add the cooked rice.
Let cool slightly and stir in the eggs, melted butter, salt
and pepper. Brown the chicken and green pepper in the
bacon fat while cooking the bacon. Remove from the bacon
fat, drain on a paper towel and add to the corn-meal-and-
rice mixture. Pour into a buttered pie tin, preferably a
pretty ceramic one, 10 inches in diameter and bake in a
400° oven until brown and crisp. Cut in wedges, split,
butter and eat out of hand. This is good for an informal
out-of-doors cocktail party where you don't mind a little
butter on your fingers. Serves 4.

CORN MEAL PANCAKES WITH CREAMED CHICKEN

These make a good light meal—for lunch or late supper or even Sunday breakfast, if that meal is for you, as it is for me, the one breakfast of the week when you eat leisurely and lavishly.

Pancake batter:

> 1 cup corn meal (either yellow or white, but
> preferably water-ground)
> 1 teaspoon salt
> 1 tablespoon sugar
> 1 egg
> ½ cup milk
> 3 tablespoons melted butter
> ½ cup flour, sifted before measuring
> 2 teaspoons baking powder

Mix the corn meal, salt and sugar and scald by pouring 1 cup of boiling water over it. Beat in the egg, milk and melted butter. Then add, with a few brisk strokes, the flour which has been resifted with the baking powder. Bake in cakes about 5 to 6 inches in diameter. Heat a small skillet of about the same size, place on it a good pat of butter and let it melt and bubble over the bottom of the pan. Put in 1 large tablespoon of the corn-meal batter so that it covers the bottom of the pan. Cook until the bubbles pop, then turn and cook on the other side. Put it aside and keep it warm while you are making the next one. Fill each of these with 1 tablespoonful of the creamed-chicken mixture given below, and fold over. Arrange on a small warm deep platter. Cover with more of the sauce and oven-brown briefly before serving.

Chicken filling:

> 2 cups diced cooked or canned chicken
> 4 tablespoons butter
> 4 tablespoons flour
> 1 cup chicken broth
> 1 cup heavy cream
> 1 jigger cognac
>   Salt, pepper

Melt the butter, blend in the flour and cook until smooth. Add the chicken broth slowly, stirring constantly until it is thickened and smooth; then add the heavy cream, salt, pepper. When that is smooth and thickened add the chicken and the cognac. Serves 4.

CURRIED CHICKEN TURNOVERS

> 1 cup ground cooked chicken
> 3 tablespoons chutney and juice
> ½ batch pie dough
> ¼ teaspoon salt
> 2 teaspoons curry powder

Grind the chicken and chutney together using the coarse blade in the meat chopper. Add salt and curry, and mix well. Roll pie dough very thin. Cut into circles 2 inches in diameter. Place a spoonful of chicken mixture on 1 side of each piece. Fold other side over and press the edges together with tines of fork. Set on baking pan and bake in a hot oven, 450°, for 5 minutes. Quickly reduce heat to moderate, 350°, and bake for about 10 to 15 minutes longer or until golden brown. Serve hot. Makes about 30 turnovers.

HOT CHICKEN SANDWICH AND FRENCH BREAD WITH OYSTER SAUCE

This is a somewhat glamorous dish that can be improvised from canned foods or leftovers in the refrigerator.

> 1 egg
> ½ cup milk
>   Salt, pepper
> 8 slices white bread
> 2 tablespoons butter
>   Sliced, cooked or canned chicken
> 3 more tablespoons butter
> 3 tablespoons flour
> 2 cups milk
>   More salt and pepper
> 1 can or jar of smoked oysters, cut in pieces, or
>   ½ cup of fresh oysters if you are not impro-
>   vising and are near a supply

Beat the egg, milk, salt and pepper together. Dip each piece of bread in this and sauté on both sides in the butter in a heavy skillet. Arrange slices of chicken between 2 pieces of the French toast and keep them warm while you make the sauce. Melt the butter, blend in the flour and add the milk slowly, stirring constantly until smooth and thick. Add seasoning, remembering that the smoked oysters have some and thus using due caution. Add the chopped smoked or fresh oysters. If you do use the fresh oysters use more seasoning. Stir until well blended and pour over the 4 sandwiches that you have arranged 1 to a warm plate. With a cucumber-and-onion salad and some freshly baked French bread, one of the partially baked varieties, this will serve 4 for a light meal.

CORN MEAL RING FILLED WITH CREAMED CHICKEN AND GREEN PEPPER

1 package corn-meal mix, mixed just slightly
damper than according to directions
¼ cup chopped onion
¼ cup grated Cheddar cheese
3 tablespoons butter
3 tablespoons flour
2 cups milk
Salt, pepper, 1 piece of bay leaf crumbled
1 teaspoon Worcestershire sauce
1 tablespoon bacon fat
1 medium-sized green pepper, finely chopped
and seeds removed
1½ cups diced cooked or canned chicken

Prepare the corn-bread mix according to directions but make it just a little more sloshy; add the onion and cheese, pour into a buttered ring mold and bake in the oven until done, which will be approximately the time given on the box or about 1 hour.

While this is baking, melt the butter in a pan, blend in the flour, add the milk, crumbled bay leaf, Worcestershire sauce, salt and pepper, and cook until smooth and thick. Brown the green pepper and the chicken in a pan with the bacon fat, and add to the sauce.

When the corn-meal mold is done, remove from the oven and unmold by running a knife gently around the edge and tapping onto a warm round plate. Pour the pepper-and-chicken sauce in the middle of the corn-meal mold and serve a wedge of mold and a spoon of sauce to each person. Serves 4.

CREAMED CHICKEN ON WAFFLES

Classic American Sunday-breakfast fare.

Waffles:

> 2 cups sifted flour
> 3 teaspoons baking powder
> 1 teaspoon sugar
> 1 teaspoon salt
> 2 cups milk
> 2 eggs, separated
> 3 tablespoons butter

Creamed chicken:

> 3 cups diced cooked chicken
> 3 tablespoons butter
> 3 tablespoons flour
> 2 cups milk
> Salt, pepper

Combine the dry ingredients and sift. Beat the egg yolks and milk together and add slowly, beating all the while, to the dry ingredients. Add the melted shortening and fold in the stiffly beaten egg whites. Fill the preheated waffle iron about ⅔ full; cover and bake until the iron stops steaming. Most waffle irons nowadays have gauges that tell you all this. These waffles are particularly good with the creamed chicken if about 3 or 4 strips of finely crumbled cooked bacon has been added to the waffle batter before baking. Makes 7 or 8 waffles.

Make the cream sauce after the waffle batter has been mixed but before the waffles are baked. Melt the butter for the cream sauce, add the flour and cook slowly until well blended. Add salt and pepper and then the milk, stirring constantly until smooth and thickened. Add the diced cooked chicken and, if wished, about 2 tablespoons of sherry. Keep this warm while you are making the waffles. Serve a tablespoon or more of the creamed chicken on each waffle.

CHICKEN THIGHS IN VERMOUTH SAUCE, WITH HEARTS OF ARTICHOKE, PIMIENTOS AND WILD RICE

2 lbs. chicken thighs or second joints,
     fresh or frozen
¼ tablespoon butter
2 tablespoons flour
1¼ cups chicken broth
¼ cup French vermouth
1 teaspoon grated lemon peel
  Salt, pepper
1 cup wild rice, cooked according to directions
     (see pages 110, 190-191)
1 No. 2 can hearts of artichoke, drained
1 can whole pimientos, cut in quarters

Sauté the chicken thighs in the butter until brown; cover and cook over a very low flame until tender. Remove from the pan and keep warm. Add the flour to the butter and juices in the pan, stir until well blended and add the broth slowly, cooking until smooth and thickened. Add the vermouth, grated lemon peel, salt and pepper. Arrange the wild rice in a shallow baking dish with pieces of chicken and pimientos and hearts of artichoke decoratively on top. Pour the vermouth sauce over all and bake in a 350° oven 20 to 30 minutes. Serves 4.

HOT CREAM PUFFS FILLED WITH CREAMED CHICKEN AND MUSHROOMS

Cream puffs:

> ¼ cup butter
> ½ cup flour, sifted before measuring
> Salt
> 2 eggs

For the cream puffs, start with everything at room temperature. Heat ½ cup water with the butter to the boiling point. Add flour and a pinch of salt. Cook the batter, stirring frequently until it leaves the sides of the pan and forms a ball. Take it off the fire and beat in the eggs 1 at a time, being careful to get one thoroughly blended before adding the other. Put spoonfuls of batter about 2 inches in diameter and about 2 inches apart on a greased cooky tin. Bake in 400° oven for ½ hour; reduce to 350° and bake 5 minutes more. To test for doneness remove 1 cream puff from the oven; if it doesn't fall they are finished. When cool, split and fill with the creamed chicken and mushrooms and heat briefly before serving.

Creamed Chicken and Mushrooms:

> ½ lb. fresh mushrooms, sliced
> 1 tablespoon butter
> 3 more tablespoons butter
> 3 tablespoons flour
> 1 cup milk
> 1 cup heavy cream
> Salt, pepper
> 1 teaspoon Worcestershire sauce
> 1 jigger sherry
> 1½ to 2 cups diced cooked or canned chicken

Sauté the fresh sliced mushroom caps in the first tablespoon of butter and their own juices until pale brown and tender. Melt the rest of the butter and stir in the flour. Cook until well blended to get rid of the floury taste. Add the milk gradually, stirring constantly, and cook until smooth and thickened. Add the heavy cream gradually and cook that, stirring until well blended with the sauce. Add salt and pepper to taste, Worcestershire sauce, sherry, mushrooms and diced cooked chicken. Serves 6.

COQUILLES DE VOLAILLE

This is just a fancy way of saying and serving creamed chicken. It is baked in scallop shells, preferably with a slice of truffle on top. However, truffles are only for "the rich and the reckless," to use Jane Nickerson's phrase referring to something else.

> 3 tablespoons butter
> 3 tablespoons flour
> 2 cups chicken broth
> 2 egg yolks, beaten with 1 tablespoon cream
>   Salt, pepper
> ⅓ cup sliced mushrooms, sautéed in butter
> 2 cups chicken, cut in small slices
> ½ cup heavy cream, whipped until stiff
>   Truffles

Melt the butter, blend in the flour, add the chicken broth slowly, stirring until thickened and smooth, remove from the fire and add the egg yolks, which have been beaten with the cream. Fold in the whipped cream, add the chicken and mushrooms, and turn into greased scallop shells. Decorate with a slice of truffle in the center of each coquille if you have the truffles; if not, forget it. Brown in a hot oven, 400°, and serve. Serves 4 to 6 in a genteel way.

OMELETTE A LA REINE WITH CREAMED CHICKEN

This is from Pierre's Restaurant in New York. He says very airily, "Make an omelette the usual way." This is my usual way:

> 4 eggs, beaten
> 4 tablespoons milk or cream
> Salt, paprika
> 2 tablespoons butter

Beat the eggs with the liquid and seasoning. Melt the butter in a skillet and when hot add the egg mixture. Cook over a very low flame, lifting the edges with a spatula or pancake turner to let the liquid run down to the bottom. When it is of fairly even consistency remove from the pan, split lengthwise and insert the creamed chicken. Decorate with slices of truffles, though naturally not on your frugal days. Serves 2 as main dish at lunch or Sunday breakfast.

Creamed chicken sauce:

> 4 tablespoons butter
> 4 tablespoons flour
> 1 cup chicken broth
> 1 cup heavy cream
> Salt, pepper
> 2 cups diced boiled chicken
> Truffles

Melt the butter, blend in the flour and add the chicken broth, slowly stirring until smooth. Then add the cream, also stirring slowly until smooth. Season and add the chicken.

VOL-AU-VENT A LA REINE

This is the way *vol-au-vent* is made and served at Henri's
—with its quiet orderly atmosphere of a more leisurely
and restrained era—in New York. It is an elegant yet un-
complicated version of chicken patty, except for the *vol-
au-vent* paste shell. Make it according to any good recipe
for puff pastry in one large oval shell with a lid or in individual shells. Or buy the shell from a good pastry shop,
ordering ahead. Somehow it's a very genteelly dramatic
way of serving chicken—very effective at a buffet dinner.

12 mushroom caps, cut in half
3 tablespoons butter
2 cups cubed boiled white meat of chicken
½ cup dry sherry (the chef says 2 glasses but
    this is what 2 sherry glasses measure)
1 pint heavy cream
2 tablespoons hollandaise sauce (it is simpler to
    use the prepared when just a bit is needed
    for the sauce)
Salt, pepper
1 large *vol-au-vent* or 4 individual ones

Sauté the mushrooms in the butter for 2 or 3 minutes. Add
the chicken and cook with the mushrooms for 2 or 3 minutes more. Pour the sherry in and let boil for a few minutes before adding the heavy cream. Let all cook for 10
minutes. Mix in 2 tablespoons hollandaise sauce and serve
in the *vol-au-vent*, which, of course, has been warmed.
Serves 4.

Puff paste according to the new *Joy of Cooking,* by Irma S.
Rombauer and Marion Rombauer Becker.

"Before beginning the adventure with puff paste there is one thing to be explained that will make its composition comparatively easy. The butter used must be washed. The purpose of washing it is to make it elastic. It should be soft through being kneaded, but in no sense soft through being melted—quite the contrary, it must be soft and cold at the same time. In winter turn on the cold water faucet. Manipulate the butter with the hands under the stream of cold water until it is creamy and waxy. At other seasons, do this in a quart of ice water placed in a bowl. The butter may be kneaded with a spoon if preferred. The final kneading of the butter is done on a board or it is patted briskly in the hands until no water flies.

"This is the recipe of a professional cook. As it calls for egg yolks it differs from the orthodox rule for puff paste. However, her results are remarkable and her method is simple, so I am giving it in preference to the usual rather complicated recipes. She stresses two points: Keep the hands, the bowl, the board and the rolling pin as cold as possible. A cold windy day is best for making puff paste.

"Work with the hands (see the first paragraph):

1 cup butter

"Place ¼ cupful of the butter in a cold bowl. Form the remainder into a square and place it where it will keep cold. Add to the butter in the bowl:

2 cups sifted all-purpose flour
¼ teaspoon salt

"Work these ingredients with a pastry blender, 2 knives or the finger-tips. Beat and add:

¼ cup ice water
2 egg yolks

"The egg yolks may be omitted. In that case use in all
6 tablespoonfuls of water. Work these ingredients well
with the hands. If necessary add, to loosen the dough
from the bowl:

A pinch of flour

"Place the dough where it will be cold but will not
freeze, preferably in the open air. If it is not possible to do
this, fold the dough in a clean cloth and place it in a dripping pan that has been placed between 2 dripping pans
filled with ice. Do not let the dough come in direct contact
with the ice. After 15 minutes, roll the dough into a square
on a floured board. Roll it one way only, not back and
forth. A good way is out from the center.

"Put the square of butter in the center of the dough and
fold the 4 corners to the center completely covering the
butter. Permit the dough to stand on a cloth or piece of
waxed paper in a cold place for ½ hour. Turn it once to
keep it from becoming dry. Roll out the dough again into
a square and fold the corners to the center. Permit it to
stand again for ½ hour. Repeat this process. The dough
must be chilled and rolled at least 4 times in all.

"Chill the dough until you are ready to use it. Wrapped
in waxed paper it may be kept in a refrigerator for several
days. Roll it, cut it into shapes [an oval, say 10 inches by 5
inches with a lid to fit]. Chill it again and bake it. One of
the success secrets of puff paste is to have it ice cold when
placed in a hot oven. The matter of baking puff paste is a
moot point. In all rules the very cold paste is put into a
very hot oven—500°. In some it is baked at this temperature throughout. In this case the pastry is covered with
waxed paper after 10 minutes' baking. In other rules the
heat is reduced 50° every 5 minutes until the temperature
is 350° for the final baking."

PUFFY BAKED OMELETTE WITH CHICKEN CURRY

A simple dish for those who think there is some occult magic known only to a few used in making an omelette.

> 2 tablespoons quick-cooking tapioca
> ¾ teaspoon salt
> ⅛ teaspoon pepper
> ¾ cup milk
> 1 tablespoon butter
> 4 egg whites
> 4 egg yolks

Mix tapioca, salt, pepper and milk together in a saucepan. Place over medium flame and cook until it comes to a boil, stirring constantly. Add butter. Take off the stove and allow to cool slightly while beating eggs.

Beat egg whites until stiff. Beat egg yolks until thick and lemon-colored. Add slightly cooked tapioca mixture and blend well. Fold into egg whites gently.

Turn into hot buttered 10-inch skillet. Cook over low heat for 3 minutes. Then bake in moderate oven, 350°, for 15 minutes. Omelette is sufficiently cooked when a knife inserted comes out clean. Cut across at right angle to handle of pan, being careful not to cut all the way through. Fold carefully from handle to opposite side and place on hot platter. Place chicken curry between folded layers and around omelette. Serve at once. Makes 4 servings.

Chicken curry:

> 1 10½-oz. can condensed cream-of-chicken soup
> ½ cup milk
> ½ to 1 or more teaspoons curry powder
> 1½ cups diced cooked chicken
> Salt and pepper

Mix cream-of-chicken soup, milk and curry powder in a saucepan. Heat, stirring occasionally. Add diced cooked chicken and season to taste. Mix and heat thoroughly. Makes about 3½ cups or 4 servings.

RENDERING CHICKEN FAT

To me the best thing about Kosher cooking that one may easily learn about in New York is the intelligent and lavish use of chicken fat. One of the most delicately flavored of all fats, it is there for the using—at least in the older chickens—and, I think, improves any dish. It gently intensifies the flavor of chicken dishes, makes the connection between eggs and chicken more plausible, and is fine in cakes and cookies. There are two ways of preparing this. This is the more traditional one:

Cut off pieces of the fatty skin and hunks of fat from a roasting or broiling chicken which has pretty lumps of yellow fat visible. Put in a heavy-bottomed pan with some cold water and cook uncovered until the water has disappeared. Add 1 chopped onion for each cup of fat in the pot. A clove of garlic may also be added, and if there is quite a lot, a chopped boiled potato will clarify the fat. The fat is done when the onion is cooked and the cracklings and the potatoes are browned. Strain and keep the fat in the refrigerator. The cracklings may be added to chopped liver or to hot breads.

My way, not the usual one, is to pull the lumps of rich yellow fat from under the skin with my fingers, put them in a pan with a small chopped onion and cook over a very slow flame until melted. Strain and use the usual ways. For cakes the onion is omitted.

STUFFED MUSHROOM CAPS

An impressive and yet simple-to-make and serve-hot hors d'oeuvre.

> 18 even-sized unblemished mushroom caps
> Melted butter
> ⅔ cup finely chopped cooked or canned chicken
> ¼ cup coarse stale homemade bread crumbs
> 3 more tablespoons melted butter
> 1 tablespoon white wine
> Salt, pepper

Brush the mushroom caps with butter—the stems you use for another dish, another day—and either sauté for 2½ minutes or put under the broiler. Mix the chopped chicken lightly with the bread crumbs, melted butter, white wine, salt and pepper. Pile into the mushroom caps, heaping somewhat. Reheat under the broiler and serve as is or on rounds of Melba toast.

SUPREME

This is served in fine French restaurants.

> 4 chicken breasts, pounded thin
> Salt, pepper
> 1 egg, beaten
> Fine homemade bread crumbs
> ½ stick butter (¼ cup)
> 1 package fresh or frozen cooked spinach
> 1 tablespoon lemon juice
> 1 tablespoon flour
> 1 cup chicken broth
> 1 teaspoon chicken bouquet
> ½ teaspoon Worcestershire sauce

4 ozs. fresh mushrooms, sliced
1 tablespoon butter

Salt and pepper the chicken breasts on both sides. Rub
lightly with the chicken bouquet and Worcestershire sauce.
Dip into the beaten egg and then into the bread crumbs.
Sauté in the ½ stick butter slowly until brown and tender,
turning from time to time. Meanwhile, melt the tablespoon
of butter in another pan and sauté the mushrooms briefly
and gently. Place the chicken breasts on the hot, cooked
spinach dressed with lemon juice, and keep warm. Add
the flour to the juices in the chicken pan and stir until
smooth. Pour over the chicken breasts and decoratively
strew the mushrooms on top. Serve very hot. Serves 4.

CREAMED CHICKEN ON HOLLAND RUSKS

1 can (12 ozs.) boned chicken, cut in large dice
1½ cups sour cream
1 teaspoon dry English mustard
1 tablespoon tarragon vinegar
Salt, pepper
1 buffet-size can hearts of artichoke, drained
4 or 8 rusks, depending on how much
bulk you want
2 tablespoons capers, well drained

Mix the chicken with the sour cream, mustard, tarragon
vinegar, salt and pepper, and heat very slowly until warm.
Do not boil or the sour cream will separate. If it does, don't
worry—it tastes all right this way; it just doesn't look so
pretty. Arrange the rusks on the plates with several hearts
of artichokes on each, and warm in the oven before pouring the chicken and sour-cream sauce over all. Sprinkle
the capers on top and serve. Serves 4.

CREAMED CHICKEN IN FLAKY PASTRY SHELLS

Make half-dollar-size shells for teas and luncheons, and even smaller ones when serving them with cocktails.

> ¼ cup finely chopped green pepper
> 1 tablespoon butter
> 1 10½-oz. can condensed cream-of-chicken soup
> ½ cup milk
> 1 cup diced cooked chicken
> ¼ cup finely chopped pimiento
> 6 baked pastry shells made from any good pie-crust recipe or ready-mix, cut to meal size (this recipe will make filling for 12 half-dollar-size shells)
> Minced parsley

Cook green pepper in butter in a saucepan. Stir in soup, then milk. Heat carefully over low heat. Add chicken and pimiento, and continue cooking about 10 minutes to blend flavors. Pour creamed chicken into pastry shells and sprinkle each with minced parsley. Makes a wonderful luncheon or dinner dish for 6.

PIMIENTOS STUFFED WITH CHICKEN HASH

This is a prettier and even healthier dish than the ubiquitous green peppers.

> 1 12-oz. can boned chicken, chopped very fine
> 4 hard-cooked eggs, chopped fine
> ½ cup mayonnaise
> Salt, pepper

3 jars whole pimientos (regular-size jar
has 3 to a jar)
Poppy seeds

Mix the chicken with the hard-cooked eggs, mayonnaise,
salt and pepper. Fill the pimientos with this, piling the
stuffing in loosely but higher than the edges of the pimientos. Sprinkle very generously with the poppy seeds, using
about 2 tablespoons in all, and bake in a 350° oven for
about 20 minutes. Serve this with something light and
filling—such as risi-pisi, an Austrian dish of cooked rice
and green peas—a green salad and hot bread. Serves 4.

VERY FANCY CHICKEN LOAF

Suitable for a late, leisurely, elegant Sunday breakfast.

3 cups diced cooked chicken
1 cup white sauce, made with 2 tablespoons
butter, 2 tablespoons flour, 1 cup broth or
milk
1 teaspoon salt
½ teaspoon pepper
1 cup mashed potatoes
1 egg
1 cup hollandaise sauce
Fresh mushroom caps

Mix the diced chicken, well seasoned with salt and pepper,
with the cream sauce. Pour into greased, decorative pottery loaf pan. Spread the top lavishly with hollandaise
sauce, either homemade or bought from a fine food store.
Mix the mashed potatoes with the egg and, using a pastry
tube, decorate the edge of the dish. Place mushroom caps
down the middle. Heat in a medium oven for 20 minutes;
place under broiler 1 or 2 minutes to brown. Serves 4.

TARRAGON CHICKEN WITH HEARTS OF ARTICHOKE AND EGGPLANT

A somewhat odd combination, inexplicably pleasing.

> 1 chicken (2½ to 3 lbs.), cut up as for frying
> 3 tablespoons butter
> 2 branches of tarragon (either fresh, which is difficult to find, or the kind that comes in jars of vinegar in fancy grocery stores)
> 1 cup chicken broth
> 1 eggplant, peeled and sliced
> Flour
> Salt, pepper
> 2 tablespoons olive oil
> 1 No. 2 can hearts of artichoke, drained and diced

Sauté the chicken in the butter until brown on all sides. Add the tarragon leaves stripped from the stems, chicken broth, salt and pepper. Cover and cook over a very low heat. Lightly flour, salt and pepper the slices of eggplant, sauté on both sides in the olive oil and drain on paper towels. Arrange the chicken in the center of a warm platter, add the juices from the pan and surround with little piles of diced artichoke interspersed with circles of the eggplant. Serves 4.

7

Oven or Pot Roasted, and Stuffed—Stuffing

CHICKEN STUFFING

To startle, impress and amuse your friends—and, of course, make a dent in your budget—fill your roast turkey with this chicken stuffing.

> 1 fricasseed chicken, cooked according to recipe
> on pages 21 and 30, skinned and diced
> Equal amount of fine homemade bread
> crumbs (5 to 7 cups)
> Salt, pepper
> 1 cup chopped onions
> ⅓ cup finely chopped parsley
> 1 to 2 cups melted butter

Mix the chicken, bread crumbs, salt, pepper, parsley and onion together. Moisten with the melted butter. Pile lightly into both the neck and body cavities of a large (16 to 22-lb.) turkey. For a smaller turkey cut the quantities in half or bake separately and roast the usual way.

ROAST CHICKEN STUFFED WITH RICE, HAM, TONGUE AND MUSHROOMS

1 roasting chicken (3½ to 5 lbs.)
1 cup uncooked rice
½ cup diced cooked ham
½ cup diced cooked tongue
½ cup mushrooms, sautéed in 1 tablespoon
    butter
2 eggs
Salt, pepper

Cook the rice with 2 cups water by bringing to a boil, then covering and turning the flame down low. Cook for 14 minutes more, at which time all the liquid will be absorbed. Let cool slightly and then mix with the ham, tongue, mushrooms, whole raw eggs, salt and pepper. Toss together gently until well mixed. Stuff the chicken and roast the usual way according to basic directions.

ROAST CHICKEN WITH A SCOTCH OAT DRESSING

This dressing has a wonderful unusual flavor and texture and will not, I promise you, taste at all like your morning cereal.

1 4 to 5-lb. roasting chicken
Salt, pepper
2 cups Scotch dry oats (American quick oats
    won't do; they get too mushy)
½ lb. melted butter
1 onion, finely chopped
1 stalk of celery, leaves and all, finely chopped
More salt and pepper

Salt and pepper the chicken inside and out. Mix the dry oats with the melted butter, onion and celery, and salt and pepper to taste. Stuff the bird with this mixture, being careful to pack it in very lightly. Roast according to basic directions until done. Serves 6.

With this type of stuffing any other starch such as rice or potatoes is unnecessary.

PATSY'S POT-ROASTED CHICKEN WITH WHITE GRAPE STUFFING

> 1 young roasting chicken (about 3 lbs., dressed weight)
> Salt
> 5 very stale slices of white bread, crumbled
> 2 small onions, chopped
> ½ teaspoon salt
> 1 teaspoon poultry seasoning
> ¾ cup white seedless grapes or other table grapes (cut ½ of the grapes into halves, leave other ½ whole)
> 1 egg beaten with 1 tablespoon water
> 4 tablespoons melted butter
> 4 more tablespoons melted butter
> 1 teaspoon summer savory

Salt the chicken inside and out. Mix together the bread crumbs, onion, salt, poultry seasoning, white grapes, beaten egg and melted butter. Stuff loosely in the chicken and skewer or sew the cavities and truss. Put the additional melted butter in the bottom of a Dutch oven and brown the chicken on all sides. Add 1 teaspoon summer savory to the butter, cover tightly and cook over a very low flame for 1½ hours, turning occasionally. Serves 3 to 4.

CHICKEN THIGHS STUFFED WITH LIVER PÂTÉ AND ONION

This is one of those recipes with a good by-product. When the bones are removed from the thighs—as second joints seem to be called these days—put them in some water with a slice of onion, some seasoning and maybe a bit of celery, and let them simmer for an hour into a flavorful stock to be used in other dishes.

> 2 lbs. fresh or frozen chicken thighs
> 2 cans of Sell's liver pâté or similar product
> 2 tablespoons minced onion
> Salt, pepper

Make a slit on the side of the thigh and cut out the bone. Mix the liver *pâté* and the chopped onion together and put a spoonful on each piece of meat. Roll and skewer closed with a toothpick, and arrange the rolls tidily in a shallow baking dish that is pretty enough to come to the table. Salt and pepper the rolls. Bake in a 350° oven about 50 minutes or until tender. Serve in the sauce, which by this time has seeped out of the meat. Serves 4.

ROAST CHICKEN STUFFED WITH PISTACHIO NUT DRESSING

This is a simple but delicate and somewhat extra-special dressing.

> 1 roasting chicken (3½ to 5½ lbs.)
> 4 cups diced white bread without crusts
> 1½ cups pistachio nuts
> 1 cup chicken broth

⅓ or more cup melted butter and chicken fat
Salt, pepper

Mix the bread, pistachio nuts, broth and melted fat together gently. Add salt and pepper with caution. The broth and sometimes the pistachios have some. The mixture should be moist but not soggy. Stuff into both cavities of the bird, being careful not to pack too tightly. Skewer or close the cavities with poultry nails or, less decoratively and less easily, sew them with string. Roast according to basic directions. Serves 4 to 6.

ROAST CHICKEN WITH CHICKEN LIVER, RICE AND TOMATO STUFFING

1 roasting chicken (3½ to 5 lbs.)
½ cup uncooked rice
2 tablespoons butter or bacon drippings
1 small onion, chopped
1 tomato, peeled and chopped
1 cup chicken broth
3 chicken livers, cut in pieces
1 tablespoon butter
1 tablespoon finely chopped parsley
Salt, pepper

Cook the rice and onion in the butter or bacon drippings until pale yellow. Add the tomato and stock, bring to a boil, cover tightly and cook over a low flame for exactly 14 minutes. Meanwhile, sauté the chicken livers in the tablespoon of butter, and add chicken livers, the butter in which they were cooked, parsley, salt and pepper to the rice mixture. Stuff bird the usual way and roast according to basic directions. Serves 6.

ROAST CHICKEN WITH KASHA, GARBANZO AND ALMOND STUFFING

This is a nutty-flavored dish—not just from the almonds. The kasha and the *garbanzos* contribute to this flavor. Serve with a cucumber-and-sour-cream salad, some hot biscuits and a substantial dessert.

> ½ cup kasha, bulgour or cracked wheat (all
>   the same thing but different grinds)
> 1 egg
> 1 cup chicken broth or water with chicken-
>   bouillon cube
> Salt
> 1 cup canned *garbanzos* or chick-peas, drained
> 1 cup chopped toasted almonds
> 1 medium-sized onion, chopped coarsely
> ¼ cup butter
> 1 chicken, ready to cook (about 3 to 3½ lbs.)
> Salt, pepper

Mix the kasha with the raw egg, stirring until all the

grains are coated. Add the bouillon and a little salt. Bring
to a boil, cover, turn the heat down low and cook 14 minutes until the liquid is absorbed and the grain dry and
fluffy. The cracked wheat will take slightly longer. Mix
with the *garbanzos*, the almonds, the onion, and add a
large lump of butter, some more salt and pepper to taste.
Salt and pepper the chicken inside and out and fill lightly
with the stuffing, being careful not to pack. Skewer the
openings with poultry nails or skewers and truss the usual
way. Place the bird on a rack in a shallow open pan and
cover with cheesecloth well saturated with melted butter.
Roast in a 350° oven about 2 hours, give or take a little.
Baste occasionally with butter. It is done when a fork
pierce in the thigh shows no pink. Serves 5 or 6.

ROAST CHICKEN WITH CORN BREAD STUFFING

> 1 chicken (3½ to 5 lbs.)
> 1½ cups crumbled corn bread, made according to
>   a basic recipe or from a good ready-mix
> 1 cup stale bread crumbs
> 1 medium-sized onion, chopped coarsely
> 1 green pepper, chopped and seeds removed
> 3 tablespoons melted butter
> 2 eggs
>   Salt, pepper
>   Chicken stock or broth

Mix the corn bread, bread crumbs, onion, green pepper,
butter, eggs, salt and pepper and enough of the chicken
broth to moisten the stuffing but not enough to make it
sloshy. Stuff loosely in the chicken cavities, being careful
not to pack. Skewer closed with poultry pins or sew. Roast
according to basic instructions. Serves 6.

POULET COCOTTE BONNE FEMME

Basically this dish in its many variations is a stuffed chicken cooked with onions, bacon and tomatoes, but the specific ingredients vary from town to town and from cook to cook.

        1 2½ to 3-lb. chicken
          Salt and pepper
        ½ lb. sausage
        2 cups bread crumbs
        1 chicken liver, chopped
        3 tablespoons finely chopped parsley
          Salt and pepper
        3 strips bacon
        3 tablespoons butter
       12 small onions
        ¼ lb. salt pork, diced
        3 medium-sized potatoes, peeled and diced

Salt and pepper the chicken inside and out. Mix the sausage, bread crumbs, chicken liver, parsley and a little more seasoning, if desired—NOT TO TASTE! NO ONE BUT AN IDIOT TASTES RAW PORK—BETTER IT'S UNDER-SEASONED. THERE'S NO CURE FOR TRICHINOSIS. Skewer the openings closed and put in a Dutch oven or an enameled iron pot and cook for 1 hour in the butter until brown on all sides.

Put the chicken down on its back and cover the breast with the bacon. Add the onions and the salt pork, cover and turn the heat very low. After about 45 minutes of cooking add the diced potatoes, stirring them around in the fat in the bottom of the pan. Cover and finish cooking in a 350° oven about 25 to 30 minutes more. Remove the bacon from the chicken and serve in the pot with the onions, potatoes and salt pork. Serves 4.

8

Rice Dishes

ARROZ CON POLLO

This is chicken with rice in any Spanish-speaking country. The versions may vary, but there are always garlic and tomatoes and onion with the chicken and rice.

> 1 2½ to 3-lb. chicken, cut up as for frying
> ½ cup olive oil
> 1 cup raw rice
> 1 medium-sized onion, chopped fine
> 1 clove garlic, minced
> 1 No. 2½ can tomatoes
> Salt, pepper

Sauté the chicken in oil until a delicate brown. Remove from the pan and keep warm. Add the rice to the oil and cook until pale yellow. Add the onion, garlic, tomatoes, chicken, salt, pepper and 1 cup of hot water. Cover and simmer for about 30 minutes or until the chicken is tender and the rice has absorbed most of the liquid. Some of the versions call for about ¼ to ½ teaspoon saffron soaked in a little water, which is delicious, tricky and very expensive. Let your pocketbook be your guide. Serves 4.

ARROZ CON VALENCIA

Arroz con valencia, or *piella,* is a chicken stew with rice and seafood—an elaborate and pretty dish that varies with the cook and the country. It is indigenous to all Spanish-speaking people. It can be as plain or fancy as you wish, but pick your colors so it's pretty.

> 2 fryers, cut up as for frying, but no wings,
>   backs or necks (that's another problem
>   for another day)
> 3 or 4 tablespoons olive oil
> 1 No. 2½ can tomatoes
> 2 hearts of celery, chopped
> 6 medium-sized onions, quartered, or
>   14 small whole ones
> 2 plump cloves garlic
>   Salt and fresh-ground pepper
> ¾ cup raw rice
> 1 lb. fresh, peeled and cleaned but not
>   cooked shrimp
> ½ lb. ham, cubed
> 1 cup fresh cooked peas
> 1 No. 2 can hearts of artichokes, drained
> 1 small can pimientos, cut in strips
> 8 well-scrubbed mussels (pretty but not
>   necessary)

Sauté the pieces of chicken in the oil until a pale, pretty brown; then add the tomatoes, celery, onions, garlic, salt, fresh-ground pepper. (Naturally this is done in your largest skillet or casserole that will take top-of-the-stove heat.) Simmer for about 45 minutes until the chicken is tender and the sauce is thick and unctuous. Add the rice and about 1 cup of boiling water, and cook for about 20 to 25

minutes or until the rice is tender. Then add the uncooked shrimp, the ham, peas, artichokes and pimientos.
The mussels, shell and all, are added at this time, too, if
you are using them. Cook for about 5 minutes, no longer.
This is enough for the seafood, and the other ingredients
are already cooked. Arrange on your prettiest platter and
serve immediately. Obviously this meal does not need to
be accompanied by anything except some good French or
Italian bread for dunking. Serves 8 generously.

ARROZ CON POLLO A LA ESPANOLA

2 broiler-sized chickens, cut up as for frying
8 small white onions
⅓ cup olive oil
3 cans tomato sauce
1 cup uncooked rice
2 lbs. mussels or clams in the shell (the mussels
     have prettier shells and prettier flesh but
     need to be very well scrubbed)
1 lb. uncooked shrimp, peeled and deveined
     Meat from 1 crab or 1 can of crab meat
⅓ cup finely chopped parsley
     Salt, pepper

Sauté the pieces of chicken in the oil with the small onions
until brown on all sides. Add the tomato sauce, rice and
1 cup of water. Cook over a low flame until the meat is
tender and the rice done, which should be about 30 minutes. Add the mussels or clams and the shrimp and crab,
and cook about 5 or 10 minutes longer until the clams are
opened and the shrimp are pink. Add salt and pepper,
sprinkle with the parsley and serve. This will serve 8
people.

CHICKEN BREASTS ON HAM WITH MUSHROOM SAUCE

This fancy dish is made from the Chicken Management recipe.

> 4 slices uncooked ham, sliced thin
> 1 cup uncooked rice
> ¼ lb. mushrooms (about 8 good caps left whole and the rest sliced thin)
> 3 tablespoons butter
> 2 tablespoons flour
> 1 cup chicken broth
> 3 tablespoons hollandaise sauce (for such a small amount it is simpler to use the fairly good kind that may be bought in jars)
> Salt, pepper
> 2 chicken breasts, carefully removed from the hen and cut in halves

Simmer the ham in water until tender. Put the rice in 2 cups water with 1 teaspoon salt, bring to a boil, cover, turn heat very low and cook for 14 minutes. Meanwhile, sauté the mushrooms, remove and keep warm. Add the flour to the butter the mushrooms have been sautéed in. Stir and slowly add the chicken broth, salt and pepper, stirring until smooth. Remove from the fire and blend in the hollandaise sauce. Divide the rice into 4 individual baking dishes, arrange a slice of ham on each, then add the chicken breasts. Add the sliced mushrooms to the sauce, pour the sauce on, top with mushroom caps and heat briefly in a 350° oven about 15 minutes. Serves 4 at a ladylike luncheon.

CHICKEN PILAU

One of the most uncluttered of the chicken-and-rice dishes.

    1 3½ to 4½-lb. chicken
    ¼ lb. salt pork, diced
    1 large onion, finely chopped
    1½ cups uncooked rice
        Salt, pepper
    2 hard-cooked eggs

Cover the chicken with water and simmer with the salt
pork, onion, salt and pepper. Simmer until the chicken is
very tender, remove the chicken from the stock, remove
the bones and cut chicken in large pieces. Put the rice in a
pan with the pieces of chicken, the salt pork and 3 cups of
the cooking liquid from the chicken. Bring to a boil, cover,
turn heat down very low and cook 14 minutes. Turn onto
a round warm platter and garnish with the yolks of the
hard-cooked eggs, which have been put through a ricer,
and the finely chopped whites of the eggs. Serves 6.

CHICKEN MOLE

Strong men and women too shudder the first time they hear or read about a mole sauce for chicken or turkey. It's a festive way of serving chicken or turkey in Mexico, but irrationally, to our way of thinking, the sauce contains chocolate. Relax; it just tastes like a smooth, hot, fiery sauce such as a curry or a creamy version of a chili sauce.

> 1 chicken (3½ to 5 lbs.), cut up as for fricassee
> 3 or 4 red or green bell peppers, cut in pieces and seeds removed
> 3 large tomatoes, peeled and chopped
> 1 cup blanched almonds
> 1 banana
> 2 2-inch sticks cinnamon
> 5 hot chili pods, toasted first and then seeds soaked in water for 1 hour
> 1 teaspoon cominos powder (cumin)
> 6 black peppercorns
> 2 teaspoons salt
> ½ cup fat
> 3 squares chocolate or ¼ Mexican chocolate, which comes in rounds, marked quarters
> 10 cloves
> 4 to 6 cups chicken broth (from the chicken)
> 1 teaspoon sugar
> 1 French roll, crumbled
> ¼ cup toasted sesame seeds

Simmer the chicken with salt in water to cover until tender. Meanwhile, sauté the tomatoes, almonds, banana, cinnamon, chili pods and soaked seeds, cominos powder, peppercorns and salt in fat. Mash very fine with mortar and pestle or other blunt instrument. Add the other ingredients; mash them. Add the strained broth from the chicken and blend well. Add the pieces of chicken, heat well and serve with some beer to quench the fire. Serves 6.

COUNTRY CAPTAIN

This dish, which is fried chicken in a curry sauce served with currants and almonds sprinkled over it, with the rice is traditionally a Southern dish or an East Indian dish, depending on who's talking. The different versions vary only in minor ingredients.

> 2 chicken (about 2½ lbs. each) cut up
>   as for frying
> Peanut oil
> 1 clove garlic, minced
> 2 large onions, chopped
> 1 No. 2½ can tomatoes
> 2 tablespoons good curry powder (not
>   grocery-store type)
> Salt, pepper
> 1 cup currants
> 1 cup sliced slivered blanched almonds
> 4 cups hot cooked rice

Sauté the pieces of chicken in the peanut oil until golden brown on all sides. Drain on paper towel and keep warm. Sauté the garlic and onion in 2 tablespoons of peanut oil. Add the tomatoes, curry powder, salt and pepper and then the pieces of chicken. Cover and simmer for about 45 minutes, adding bouillon or water if it starts to dry out. Tomatoes vary in their juiciness. To serve arrange the hot rice around the edge of a large warm platter, pour the chicken mixture in the center and sprinkle the currants over the rice and the almonds over all. Serves 6.

CHICKEN RISOTTO

Once you have cooked rice the Italian way, which is, as a matter of fact, the way of most of the Mediterraneans, boiled rice will seem extremely flat and tasteless, and of course it is unless given some positive flavoring.

3 tablespoons olive oil
1 clove garlic, minced
1 onion, chopped fine
1 can Italian tomato paste
1 No. 2½ can tomatoes
    Salt, pepper
1 teaspoon basil
¼ cup butter
1 2½ to 3-lb. chicken
¼ lb. more butter
1 cup uncooked rice
2 cups of the stock the chicken is cooked in
    Pinch saffron (if you are feeling lavish,
        soak in a bit of the broth)
1 more small onion, chopped very fine

This is the night that you are cooking on all burners. Make a good tomato sauce to serve with the rice and chicken, because the rice will have absorbed all the liquid and will be flavorful but dry and flaky. Sauté the onion and garlic in the olive oil until pale yellow. Add the tomato paste, tomatoes, salt, pepper and basil, and simmer until thick and flavorful. Depending on the way that you feel about this, it can take from 45 minutes to 2 hours. Serve in a separate bowl. Meanwhile, salt and pepper the chicken and sauté in the butter until golden brown on all sides.

Cover tightly and cook over a very low flame until tender, maybe 25 to 30 minutes. Arrange on a platter and keep warm. About 20 minutes before the chicken is done melt the next batch of butter and stir the rice around in it until each grain is pale yellow and glistening. Then add the minced onion and stir in the butter until that too is pale yellow. Add the stock, bring to a boil, cover and cook 15 minutes. Arrange around the chicken. Spoon the tomato sauce over each serving. Serves 4.

CHICKEN JAMBALAYA

The New Orleans stew that is apt to include a little bit of everything, and in New Orleans that usually includes some seafood along with the chicken.

>2 tablespoons lard
>1 tablespoon flour
>1 No. 2½ can tomatoes
>1 cup rice
>1 onion, chopped
>½ green pepper, chopped
>1 red-pepper pod
> Salt, pepper
>2 cups diced cooked chicken
>1 lb. raw shrimp, peeled and deveined
>1 pint oysters

Melt the lard, stir in the flour, add the tomatoes and cook until smooth. Add the rice, onions, green pepper, chicken, red pepper, salt and pepper. Simmer for about 20 minutes or until the rice is tender. Add the shrimp and oysters and cook for not more than 5 minutes more. Serves 4 to 6.

CHICKEN SMITANE ACCORDING TO CAFÉ ST. DENIS

Made with either chicken or guinea hen and wild rice. This is usually one of the most expensive ways of getting chicken in a fancy French restaurant. There doesn't seem to be too much reason why it should be so costly except for the wild rice (which of course is very, very expensive). The preparation is not too complicated.

> 2 young broilers (1½ to 2 lbs.), boned and
>   the bones saved for stock
> 1 medium-sized onion, chopped
> 1½ tablespoons butter
> ⅓ cup white wine
> 2 cups chicken broth
>   Dash of thyme
> 1 bay leaf
> 2 tablespoons butter
> 1 cup wild rice, washed in many waters
> 1 cup sour cream
>   Juice of 1 lemon
>   Salt, pepper

Cut the broilers in halves or quarters and take the bones out as carefully as possible. This is not so difficult as removing them from a whole chicken, leaving it more or less intact. Brown the bones with the onion in the butter and pour in the white wine, 2 cups of chicken broth, thyme and bay leaf and simmer for 1 hour. The liquid should be reduced to about ⅔ of the previous amount. Meanwhile, sauté the boned broilers for about 12 or 15 minutes, browning well on both sides, and cook the wild rice in a pan with

2½ cups of water and 1 teaspoon of salt. Bring to a boil, cover and cook over a very low heat until the rice is flaky and dry, which should be about 40 to 60 minutes. Drain if necessary, though the water should have cooked away. Strain the broth that the bones have been cooking in. This should be considerably reduced—sort of a distilled essence of chicken. Add the sour cream and the lemon juice. Let this warm but not cook, and pour it over the chicken quarters or halves, which have been arranged on plates on a bed of wild rice. Serves 4.

CHICKEN AND WALNUT PILAF

>   2 cups cooked chicken (preferably roasted
>   rather than boiled), cut in large pieces
>   ½ cup coarsely diced onion
>   3 tablespoons butter
>   ½ teaspoon thyme
>   Salt, pepper
>   1 cup uncooked rice
>   2 cups chicken broth (chicken bouillon cubes
>   dissolved in boiling water may be used)
>   ½ can Italian tomato paste
>   ⅓ cup coarsely diced walnuts

Brown the chicken and the onion in the fat in a deep, heavy skillet, add the rice and seasoning and stir until slightly colored. Add the chicken broth and tomato paste, bring to a boil, cover and turn the flame down very low. Cook for 14 minutes, at which time the liquid should be all absorbed. Add the walnuts and serve with corn bread and bitter green salad. Serves 4.

CURRIED CHICKEN AND SHRIMP

1 cup moist grated coconut
2 cups bouillon
1 lb. uncooked shrimp, peeled and deveined
2 tablespoons butter
1 chicken (about 2½ lbs.), cut up as for frying
3 tablespoons butter
2 tablespoons flour
  Salt, pepper
2 tablespoons curry powder
  Hot cooked rice
  Chutney
  Hearts of palm, sliced
  Cooked crumbled bacon
  Guava jelly, or what you will

Warm the coconut slightly in the bouillon but do not cook. Cook the shrimp in the 2 tablespoons of butter 3 to 5 minutes and stop when they get pink. Set them aside. Sauté the chicken in the other 3 tablespoons butter until brown on all sides; then cover and cook over a low flame until tender. Transfer the chicken and the shrimp to a warm platter and keep hot.

Make a sauce, using the butter in the shrimp pan and the butter and juices in the chicken pan, and stir in the flour, blending until smooth. Add salt, pepper and curry powder, and then slowly add the coconut and bouillon, stirring until thickened and smooth except for the coconut. Simmer the sauce for ½ hour, then add the shrimp and chicken. Cook for 15 minutes more so that the flavors are well intermingled. Serve on a platter surrounded by the rice, with the chutney, the hearts of palm, the bacon and the Guava jelly in small separate bowls. Serves 4.

PIERRE'S FRICASSEE OF CHICKEN ON RICE

This is also from Hubert Krenn, the chef at Pierre's Restaurant, in New York.

> 1 chicken (3½ to 4 lbs.), cut up as for fricassee
> 1 onion with 3 cloves in it
> 3 stalks celery, cut in pieces
> 2 bay leaves
> 2 cups uncooked rice
> ¼ lb. butter
> ¼ cup chopped onions
> 4 cups chicken bouillon
> 2 more tablespoons butter
> 1 tablespoon flour
> 2 cups chicken broth
> ½ cup heavy cream
> Salt, pepper

Almost cover the chicken with water, and simmer the onion—stuffed with the cloves—celery, bay leaves, salt and pepper for 2½ to 3 hours or until tender. About 20 minutes before the chicken seems to be done—it will be almost tender by this time—slowly cook the rice and chopped onions in the butter until pale yellow and glistening. Add the 4 cups of chicken bouillon. Bring to a boil, cover, turn heat down and cook for 16 minutes. At the same time start the sauce by melting the 2 tablespoons of butter and cooking with the flour for 3 or 4 minutes. Add the chicken broth and cook slowly until thickened. Add the heavy cream. When the chicken is done, skin and cut the meat from the bone. Place on the rice when cooked. Pour the sauce over it. Heat together briefly and serve. Serves 4 to 6 generously.

CHICKEN AND RICE WITH AN EGG CRUST

>   1 2½ to 3-lb. chicken, cut up as for frying
>   1½ cups rice
>   1 egg yolk
>   Salt, pepper
>   ⅓ cup finely chopped parsley
>   ⅓ cup butter

Cook the chicken, with salt and pepper, in about 2 quarts of water until tender. Then cook the rice in 3 cups of this liquid in another pan, bringing to a boil, covering and cooking over a very low flame for 14 minutes or until all the liquid is absorbed. Arrange ½ the rice in a shallow, buttered baking dish with the pieces of chicken. Top with the rest of the rice and pat smooth with a spoon. Beat the egg yolk with 3 tablespoons of the liquid the chicken was cooked in, and pour over the rice-and-chicken mixture. Sprinkle with the parsley and dot with the butter. Put in a 350° oven for 20 to 25 minutes or until the top is browned and crusted. Serves 4 to 6.

CHICKEN SOUFFLÉ WITH RICE AND A FEW OTHER THINGS

This is somewhat more substantial than the usual soufflé.

>   3 tablespoons butter
>   3 tablespoons flour
>   1 cup heavy cream
>   Salt and pepper
>   3 eggs, separated
>   1 cup cooked rice
>   1 cup diced cooked or canned chicken
>   ⅓ cup finely chopped ham

1 small onion, finely chopped
½ cup grated Swiss or Parmesan cheese

Melt the butter, blend in the flour and add the cream slowly, cooking until smooth and thickened. Remove from the
fire and stir in the egg yolks and then the rice, chicken,
ham, onion and cheese. Whip the egg whites until stiff and
fold in gently. Turn into a greased baking dish, preferably
one with straight sides, and bake in a 350° oven until the
top is lightly browned and springs back when gently
touched with the finger. Serves 4 to 6.

GREEK CHICKEN WITH RICE

1 ready-to-cook young chicken (2½ to 3 lbs.),
   cut up as for frying
½ cup butter
1 medium-sized onion, chopped
1 teaspoon salt
¼ teaspoon black pepper
1 6-oz. can tomato paste
½ teaspoon sugar
1 cup rice
¼ cup butter

Melt the butter in a pan, add the chicken and sauté until
it is a pretty brown. Add onion, salt, pepper, tomato paste,
sugar and 2 or 3 tablespoons of water. Cover and cook
gently until the chicken is barely tender. Add 3 cups of
boiling water and sprinkle rice over the top. Cover again
and steam until the rice is tender and most of the liquid
absorbed, about 15 minutes. Arrange on a serving dish.
Melt remaining ¼ cup butter in the cooking pan and pour
over the rice and chicken. Serves 4 or 5.

ED'S EASY ONE-DISH MEAL

A bland simple dish that may be, but wasn't, prepared from the kitchen cabinet by an unhousebroken man.

> 1 cup rice (use precooked if you wish)
> 1 can (12 ozs.) boned chicken, diced
> 1 cup cooked or canned peas (½ frozen
>   package)
> 1 10½-oz. can undiluted condensed cream-of-
>   chicken soup
> Salt, pepper, with caution (soup has some)
> Grated cheese

Put 1 cup of rice in 2 cups of water and bring to a boil. Cover and cook over a very low flame for 14 minutes, or use the precooked rice according to directions. Arrange in a casserole with the diced chicken and the peas on top. Spoon the soup over this, add a little seasoning and sprinkle the top with the grated cheese. Put in a 350° oven 15 or 20 minutes or until the top is brown and bubbling. Serves 4.

FRENCH PILAF

This is the French version of Country Captain that turns up as a regional dish practically everywhere.

> 1 3-lb. chicken, cut up as for fricassee
> Salt, pepper
> 1½ cups uncooked rice
> 1 tablespoon or more curry powder
> ¼ cup butter

    1 cup blanched almonds, cut in slivers
    1 cup white seedless raisins

Put the chicken into 2½ quarts of water with salt and pepper, and simmer over a low flame 1 to 1½ hours or until the chicken is tender. Remove from the broth and keep warm. Add 3 cups of chicken broth and curry powder to the rice, bring to a boil, cover, turn heat down very low and cook 14 minutes. Add the butter, almonds and raisins. Arrange the rice on a warm deep platter with the pieces of chicken on top. Serves 6.

ARMENIAN PILAF

    1 cup uncooked rice
    ¼ cup pistachios or slivered almonds (or a
        mixture of both)
    2 tablespoons olive oil
    2½ cups chicken broth
    ¼ cup fine Armenian *pasta,* which looks like
        rice, or broken bits of uncooked
        Armenian spaghetti
    3 cups boiled chicken, cut in pieces
    Salt, pepper

Cook the rice in the olive oil with the almonds and pistachios until the nuts are slightly brown and the rice is pale yellow. Add the *pasta,* broth, chicken and seasoning, bring to a boil, cover tightly and cook over a very low heat until the liquid is absorbed, about 14 to 15 minutes. Serve with a colorful and somewhat acid salad, such as tomato aspic with hearts of artichoke embedded in it, and corn muffins—neither of which are Armenian. Serves 4.

CURRIED CHICKEN WITH PINEAPPLE CHUNKS AND BRAZIL NUTS

3 tablespoons butter
2 cloves garlic, chopped fine
1 small onion, chopped
1 small apple, chopped fine
3 tablespoons flour
2 tablespoons good strong curry powder
2 cups chicken broth (preferably homemade or canned)
1 cup heavy cream
2 cups cooked chicken, cut in large dice (canned chicken is characterless in this recipe)
1 package frozen pineapple chunks or 1 cup fresh ones that have been sugared and chilled
⅔ cup slivered toasted Brazil nuts
Hot flaky rice

Cook the garlic, onion and apple in the butter until pale yellow and partially cooked. Sprinkle with the flour and curry powder and stir around until blended. Add the chicken broth, stirring constantly until thickened. Add the cream slowly, stirring until that too is thickened, then add the chicken. Let stand in the sauce, preferably overnight in the refrigerator to let the flavors "ripen" as it were. Before serving heat the sauce and serve with hot flaky rice accompanied by the cold pineapple chunks and the toasted Brazil-nut chips. The Brazil nuts may be sliced easily by dropping in boiling water first. Serves 4.

CURRIED CHICKEN PILAU

2 lbs. chicken breasts
2 tablespoons good fresh curry powder
1 cup uncooked rice
    Salt
¼ lb. butter

Poach the chicken breasts in 2½ cups water with the curry powder and salt. This may be done either on top of the stove or in a 350° oven 40 to 50 minutes. Cook the rice in the butter until pale yellow, then put in a baking dish with the pieces of chicken and 2 cups of the cooking liquid. Add some salt and cook in a 350° oven 20 to 30 minutes or until the liquid is absorbed. Add more liquid if the rice begins to dry out before it is tender. Serves 4.

9

Salads

AVOCADO WITH CHICKEN SALAD

Sometimes the simplest ways are really the best. Certainly this needs no embellishment if given the best ingredients, a hot but pleasant day, the right company and a glass of cold, dry, white wine.

2 large ripe avocados, cut in half
2 cups home-roasted or boiled chicken, cut
    in pleasantly positive cubes
½ cup homemade or very best mayonnaise
    you can buy
Salt

Toss the chicken lightly with the mayonnaise and pile generously in the avocado halves. There are some who like an occasional piece of chilled grapefruit segment in this, but this is one of those recipes where I think you should leave well enough alone. Serves 4.

CHICKEN MOUSSE CHABLIS

Rich, velvety and fattening and well worth the bulges and the bother.

1 envelope unflavored gelatin
½ cup California Chablis or other white
table wine
3 egg yolks
¾ cup chicken broth (canned or bouillon-
cube broth may be used)
1 cup ground cooked chicken
2 tablespoons chopped parsley
1½ teaspoons lemon juice
1 teaspoon onion juice
Salt, celery salt and paprika to taste
Dash of cayenne
1 cup heavy cream, whipped until stiff

Soften gelatin in the wine. Beat egg yolks slightly in top of a double boiler. Add chicken stock and cook over hot water, stirring constantly, until mixture thickens. Remove from heat. Add softened gelatin and stir until dissolved. Add chicken, parsley, lemon juice, onion juice, salt, celery salt, paprika and cayenne. Chill until mixture begins to thicken, then fold in whipped cream. Turn into a 1-quart mold or individual molds lightly brushed with salad oil. Chill until firm. Serves 4 to 6.

Unmold on a party platter and serve surrounded by halves of deviled eggs, asparagus tips and quarters of tomatoes, or mold in a ring and fill the center with mayonnaise mixed with coarsely chopped walnuts. Black walnuts now available almost everywhere in cans are fine if you care for their odd acrid flavor.

CHEF'S SALAD

The exact ingredients for a chef's salad is a matter for argument. What I want when I order one in a restaurant is this:

> 1½ cups chicken, both white and dark meat, cut julienne fashion
> ¾ cup ham, cut julienne fashion
> ¾ cup Switzerland Swiss cheese
> Greens
> French dressing (2 parts olive oil, 1 part red-wine vinegar, salt and fresh-ground black pepper)

Lightly toss together the chicken, ham, cheese and greens that have been torn with the fingers. Mix the dressing and pour over the salad, tossing gently but thoroughly some more until all is well moistened. Serves 4, with hot rolls for lunch or Sunday-night supper.

CHICKEN AND CUCUMBER MOUSSE

> 1 package unflavored gelatin
> ¼ cup lemon juice
> 1¾ cups chicken broth
> 1 cup mayonnaise
> 1 small onion, chopped fine
> 1 medium-sized cucumber, peeled and chopped fine
> 1½ cups diced cooked chicken
> 2 tablespoons chives (good dried ones may be bought now in fancy grocery stores)
> Water cress

Soften the gelatin in the lemon juice. Heat the chicken broth and add the softened gelatin and lemon juice. Stir until dissolved. Let cool slightly; fold in the mayonnaise, onion, cucumber, chicken and chives. Turn into a mold that has been rinsed with cold water or very lightly brushed with a flavorless salad oil. Put in the refrigerator and chill until firm. Unmold on a bed of water cress and serve. Needs no other dressing because the dressing is built in. Serves 4.

COLD CHICKEN BALLS

Cold chicken in a pleasing and different guise.

>1 envelope unflavored gelatin
>Juice of ½ medium-sized lemon
>1 cup hot chicken broth or stock
>3 cups diced cooked or canned chicken
>Salt, pepper
>3 hard-cooked egg yolks, chopped fine
>⅓ cup finely chopped parsley

Soften the gelatin in the lemon juice and dissolve in the hot chicken broth. Add the diced chicken and seasoning and chill until somewhat thickened. Make into balls, the size varying according to how they are served. As a luncheon or light supper dish make them about the size of walnuts in the shells or even larger. To serve with cocktails, make them about the size of marbles. Roll them in the chopped egg yolks and parsley mixed together, and chill until needed. Serves 4 for a light meal with an avocado-and-tomato-aspic salad and hot bread. For cocktail parties there is no guessing—things vary so according to the guests, how long they stay and what else you are serving.

CHICKEN ROLL

A complicated and elegant sublimation of a chicken loaf.

> 4 cups ground uncooked chicken
> 1 cup dry bread crumbs
> 1 medium-sized onion, chopped very fine
> ½ cup chopped walnuts
> 2 teaspoons salt
> ½ grated nutmeg
> 2 whole eggs
> 2 quarts chicken broth or the bones of the
>   chicken with celery, onion, bay leaf and
>   seasoning brought to a boil

Mix the raw meat in a bowl with the bread crumbs, onions, walnuts and seasoning, using your fingers to make sure that it is all intermingled. Add the whole eggs and mix thoroughly with your fingers. Pat into a neat even roll 3 to 4 inches in diameter and roll up in a piece of cheese-cloth. Tie the ends and sew or pin the sides together symmetrically. Put in the pot with the broth, or the broth that is in the making, and cook slowly for about 2 or 2½ hours. Remove from the broth and chill. Slice and serve on a platter with the slices overlapping in a circle on a bed of water cress. Surround this with pickled mushrooms and Belgian carrots that have been marinated in a good vinaigrette dressing, chilled and drained. Tiny, tender and prettily symmetrical imported Belgian carrots come in expensive cans. Serves 4 to 6.

CHICKEN SALAD WITH CUCUMBERS, WATER CHESTNUTS AND WALNUTS

This is an especially fresh and clean-tasting version.

> 3 cups diced cooked or canned chicken
> ½ large cucumber, peeled and diced

½ cup thinly sliced water chestnuts
⅓ cup coarsely chopped English walnuts or ¼
    cup black walnuts (the black walnuts are
    for those who like their acrid positive
    flavor)
1 cup mayonnaise
Salt, pepper
Crisp greens

Toss all the ingredients together in the order in which they are listed and bed down on the crisp greens. Serves 4.

VERY SPECIAL CHICKEN SALAD

For a very, very special chicken salad that can be made ahead of time roast the chicken instead of boiling. This gives it better flavor and texture.

3 cups diced roast chicken
1 package frozen pineapple chunks or better,
    but less simply, 1 cup fresh diced pineapple
2 tablespoons red-wine vinegar
2 tablespoons olive oil
    Salt, fresh-ground black pepper
⅓ cup mayonnaise, thinned slightly with
    tarragon vinegar
2 tablespoons toasted slivered almonds
    Crumbled bacon (nice but not obligatory)
    Greens

Mix chicken, pineapple, vinegar, olive oil and seasoning. Chill. Just before serving mix with the slightly thinned mayonnaise and sprinkle with almonds and bacon. Serve on crisp greens. Serves 4.

CHICKEN SALAD WITH AVOCADO

Delicate and colorful and different. The chicken may be boiled if wished, but the flavor is more positive when roasted.

1 chicken (3 to 3½ lbs.), ready to cook
6 ripe avocados
3 tablespoons lemon juice
2 tablespoons salad oil
⅓ cup chopped toasted almonds
3 tablespoons peeled white grapes
Dash red pepper
Salt

Roast chicken according to basic directions. Let cool, pull meat from the bones and dice coarsely. Add white grapes, peeled and halved, and well-buttered toasted almonds. Scoop out the center pulp of 6 thoroughly ripe avocados. Slice thin or chop enough of the pulp to make approximately ⅓ cupful. Add this to the chicken mixture. Mash about ¼ of the remaining avocado pulp with a fork; add lemon juice, salt and red pepper. Beat with a fork until light and fluffy, slowly adding salad oil as needed to make a creamy consistency. Combine avocado dressing with other ingredients and toss lightly. Fill scooped avocado shells with the salad mixture. Sprinkle with white grapes and almonds. Serves 6.

CHICKEN SALAD WITH HARD-COOKED EGG YOLK DRESSING

On a hot summer day when appetites are capricious there is nothing better than a delicate and good chicken salad such as this, with a dressing made of the very essence of the chicken, and nothing worse than a dull and indifferent one slapped together carelessly.

> 3 cups coarsely cut cooked chicken
> 1½ cups chopped celery
> 4 hard-cooked egg yolks, mashed
> Sufficient chicken broth to moisten
> Salt, pepper, paprika to taste
> Finely chopped hard-cooked egg whites
> for garnish

Mix the diced cooked chicken gently with the celery in order not to mash. Mix the egg yolks with the chicken broth until it has nice consistency for a dressing, and add the amount of seasoning that suits your family. Spoon over the chicken and celery. Cover and chill in the refrigerator until ready to serve. Serve on a bed of crisp water cress and sprinkle the top with the chopped egg whites. Serves 4.

CHICKEN AND SWEETBREADS SALAD WITH BLANCHED AND SAUTÉED ALMONDS

2 cups diced cooked chicken
1 pair diced cooked sweetbreads
Salt
1 cup mayonnaise
Water cress
⅔ cup slivered blanched almonds sautéed
in a little butter

Mix the chicken with the sweetbreads, salt, mayonnaise, and ½ of the almonds. Chill until ready to serve. Just before serving put on a bed of water cress and sprinkle with the rest of the almonds. To blanch the almonds drop them in boiling water for a few minutes, then drain, plunge into cold water and slip off the skins. Cut the almonds lengthwise into halves, brown in 2 teaspoons of butter and add a little salt. Serves 4.

CHICKEN MOUSSE

2 tablespoons (or envelopes) plain
unflavored gelatin
2 cups hot well-seasoned chicken stock
or bouillon
1 teaspoon salt, approximately
⅛ teaspoon pepper
1 teaspoon paprika
½ teaspoon Worcestershire sauce
1 teaspoon grated onion
2 cups finely diced chicken
½ cup finely chopped celery
¼ cup finely chopped green pepper

½ cup nonfat dry milk
1 teaspoon lemon juice

Soften the gelatin in ½ cup cold water in mixing bowl for about 5 minutes. Pour hot stock or broth over gelatin and stir until dissolved. Stir in salt, pepper, paprika, Worcestershire sauce and onion. Chill until mixture begins to thicken. Add chicken, celery and green pepper, mixing well. Over the top of ½ cup of water, sprinkle the dry milk powder and beat with rotary beater or electric mixer until stiff, about 10 minutes by hand. Gradually beat in lemon juice and beat 5 minutes longer. Fold gently into gelatin mixture. Pour into 5-cup ring mold. Chill until firm. Unmold on chilled platter. Garnish with water cress or broken chicory leaves. Serves 6.

ROAST CHICKEN IN TARRAGON JELLY

1 package unflavored gelatin
¼ cup tarragon vinegar
1¾ cups strong rich chicken broth (which means
no cubes this time)
Salt and pepper if needed
Slices of white and dark roasted chicken (be
as lavish as you wish; there should be at
least 3 long slanting slices for each person)

Soften the gelatin in the tarragon vinegar, heat the chicken broth and dissolve the softened gelatin in it, adding seasoning if needed. Arrange the slices of chicken in nice overlapping slices in a mold that has been rinsed with cold water. Pour the gelatin mixture over it. Chill until firm. Unmold and serve on a bed of water cress. Sprinkle the molded chicken with a few capers, but do not sully it by any such superfluities as mayonnaise. Serves 4.

PRESSED CHICKEN PIMIENTO

As old-fashioned as a church supper, with the same warm and familiar appeal.

> 2 chickens (2½ to 3½ lbs.)
> 2 envelopes unflavored gelatin
> 3 or 4 canned pimientos, sliced
> 3 cups boiling chicken stock
>   Salt, pepper
> 2 hard-cooked eggs (nice but not obligatory)

Simmer chicken until tender in just enough water to cover. Remove skin and separate meat from bones. Slice meat from breast and chop the rest. Chill. Skim fat from broth and season rather lavishly with salt and pepper. Cook until reduced to 3 cups, then strain. Soften gelatin in ½ cup cold water, add to condensed broth and stir until dissolved. Cover bottom of a 2-qt. loaf pan, or mold rinsed in cold water, with ⅛-inch layer of prepared broth. Chill till set. Arrange pimiento slices and sliced eggs prettily; then arrange sliced white meat to make an even layer. Cover lightly with broth and chill until firm. Cool, then chill remaining broth till sirupy. Add the rest of the chicken, the pimientos and chopped eggs to the broth, and pack into mold or pan. Chill until firm. Unmold on a platter and garnish with water cress or lettuce leaves and sliced hard-cooked eggs. Slice or cut into squares and serve as a main dish on a hot day. Serves 8 to 12.

CURRIED CHICKEN SALAD SPRINKLED WITH WHITE GRAPES AND CRUMBLED BACON

There is no law that says chicken salad must be forever bland and forever dull. This one, easily concocted from cooked or canned chicken, has a refreshing difference and piquancy and yet will not frighten conservative eaters.

> 3 cups coarsely diced cooked or canned chicken (12-oz. can)
> 1 cup mayonnaise (*not* salad dressing)
> 1 tablespoon or more good curry powder (that means avoid the grocery-store type if possible)
> Salt, white pepper
> Crisp greens
> ⅓ lb. white seedless grapes, washed, stripped from the stems and chilled
> 3 slices bacon, cooked until crisp just before needed, and drained well

Put the chicken in a bowl. Add the mayonnaise mixed to taste with the curry powder, salt and white pepper. Cover, and chill together for at least 1 hour. If not covered the mayonnaise will turn brown around the edges and sometimes liquefy. When ready to serve transfer to a decorative bowl or platter, surround with greens, sprinkle the white grapes and then the crumbled, slightly warm bacon on top.

RING MOLD OF CHICKEN

1 package lemon-flavored gelatin
2 cups hot chicken stock, free from fat
1 cup diced cooked chicken
½ cup chopped celery
¼ cup chopped green pepper
2 tablespoons chopped pimiento
2 tablespoons vinegar
¼ teaspoon salt
½ cup cooked peas
1 teaspoon grated onion
Pepper
Dash of Worcestershire sauce

Dissolve the gelatin in the hot chicken stock. Chill until about as thick as uncooked egg white. Combine remaining ingredients and fold into the slightly thickened gelatin. Turn into greased ring mold. Chill until firm. Unmold and serve on crisp lettuce. Garnish with mayonnaise. Serves 4.

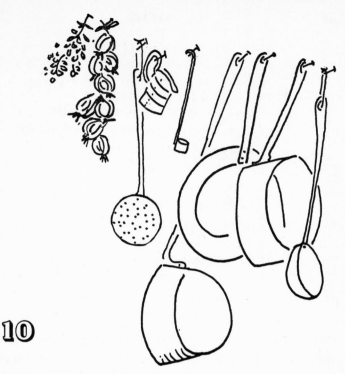

10

Soups

CHICKEN AND OYSTER BROTH

Light and festive.

> 4 cups chicken broth
> 1 pint oysters and their liquor
> ½ cup heavy cream
> Salt, paprika

Heat the chicken broth, add the oysters and cook until the edges of the oysters begin to curl or ruffle. Have the cream stiffly whipped and seasoned with the salt and paprika. Put a spoonful in each bowl and pour in the consommé-and-oyster mixture. Serves 4.

CHICKEN GUMBO

The New Orleans soup that is a meal in itself, and is so infinitely varied that the only sure things are that it will be hotly seasoned, that there will be okra and/or gumbo filé—a seasoning made from sassafras—and that it always will be served with a separate bowl of flaky cooked rice to spoon into it.

        1 tablespoon flour
        1 tablespoon lard
        1 onion, chopped fine
        1 3 to 3½-lb. chicken, cut in pieces
        ½ lb. diced ham
        1 red-pepper pod
        ½ teaspoon thyme
        1 tablespoon parsley
        1 No. 2½ can tomatoes
        1 lb. okra (leave small pods whole but slice the
            older ones)
        2 tablespoons gumbo filé powder
        Salt, pepper
        Hot cooked rice

Cook slowly, stirring the lard and flour together until slightly colored. Add the onion and when it is partly cooked but before it is brown, add the chicken and cook slowly, turning over and over until the chicken is well browned. Add the ham, red pepper, thyme, parsley and tomatoes, and put into a soup pot with 1½ pints of boiling water and the okra. Cover and cook slowly for about 3 hours. If the okra is unobtainable, and if you prefer, add 2 tablespoons of the filé powder just before serving. The filé is NEVER, NEVER cooked. This may be varied in other ways. Shrimp or oysters may be added, the tomatoes may be omitted, and so on. Serves 4 to 6.

MULLIGATAWNY

This is the classic curried soup of India, always served with a bowl of flaky rice so that each person may put a spoonful in his soup bowl.

> 1 chicken (3½ to 4 lbs.), cut in pieces
> 2 tablespoons butter
> 1 small onion, chopped
> 1 small apple, chopped
> 1 to 2 tablespoons good strong curry powder
> 6 cups veal or chicken stock
>   Salt, pepper
>   Lemon juice
>   Hot rice

Sauté the chicken in the butter in the bottom of a Dutch oven. Add the onion, apple and curry powder, and stir around until well blended and the onion and apple are partially cooked. Add the stock and seasoning and simmer for about 1½ to 2 hours. Remove the chicken and skim off the fat while hot, blotting the grease with paper towels, using one at a time and throwing it away as it has absorbed the grease and starting with a fresh one. Or chill and spoon the solidified fat from the top. Strain and reheat with the pieces of chicken. Serve with a piece of chicken and rice in each bowl. Serves 4 to 6 generously.

CREAM OF CHICKEN ALMOND SOUP

¾ cup blanched ground almonds
4 cups chicken stock
3 tablespoons butter
3 tablespoons flour
1 cup heavy cream
Salt
White pepper

Simmer the almonds with the chicken broth slowly for about 1 hour and rub through a fine sieve. Melt the butter, stir the flour into it and gradually add the hot strained soup. Boil together for a few minutes and add the salt, white pepper and heavy cream, which has been slightly heated. Beat slightly with a rotary beater to get a smooth well-blended soup. Serves 4.

COCK-A-LEEKIE SOUP

This is a traditional Scotch dish. The prunes are a rational
and usual ingredient no matter how odd they may sound
to our ears.

> 2 large bunches of leeks (white part only), cut
> in 1-inch lengths and then into halves
> lengthwise
> 1 rooster (cock) or fowl (somewhat aged)
> Beef or veal stock
> Salt and pepper
> 12 prunes

Wash the leeks very carefully as they are apt to be sandy.
Simmer the leeks and the fowl in the beef or veal stock,
which should be ample—about 3 quarts—for 3½ to 4
hours. A half hour before finishing, add the whole prunes.
Transfer the rooster or fowl to a hot tureen and cut up into
serving pieces. Remove the fat from the top of the soup
by putting an ice cube in a piece of cloth and swishing it
around just under the surface of the soup so that it will
collect the rising fat; or chill the soup and then remove the
grease; or blot it from the top while still hot with a paper
towel, repeating with a fresh towel until all the grease is
removed. Pour the strained hot broth over it, add the
prunes and serve. Serves 4 to 6.

CHICKEN STOCK

Even in these days of short cuts, canned bouillon, and
bouillon cubes there is something very satisfying and
rewarding in both the making and the using of a good
homemade chicken broth. The long cuts really are better
but there must be the time, energy and wish to use them.

Of course even this is cheating somewhat by using the pressure cooker.

> 3 lbs. chicken (these may be necks, wings and backs, purchased cheaply in stores that sell separate parts)
> ½ cup chopped carrots
> ½ cup chopped celery
> ½ cup chopped onion
> Salt
> About 1 dozen peppercorns

Put the chicken in the pressure cooker with 2 quarts of water. Bring to a boil slowly in the uncovered cooker. Skim, add the vegetables, cover and bring up to 15 lbs. pressure and cook for 30 minutes longer. Let the pressure go down naturally. Cool, chill, skim off the fat and strain through cheesecloth. Store in covered jars in refrigerator until needed. This may be frozen in containers each holding a cup—a convenient measure—for future use.

ROAST CHICKEN OR CARCASE SOUP

A different consistency from the usual chicken soup but pleasing in its own way, with an interesting flavor, and, of course, very frugal.

> 1 roast chicken carcase
> 1 medium-sized onion, chopped
> 2 stalks celery, cut in pieces
> 1 dozen peppercorns
> 2 teaspoons salt
> 1 teaspoon Worcestershire sauce
> Giblets and the neck, except for the liver

Put in a pressure cooker with 2 quarts water, making sure that with the other ingredients added the pan is not more than ⅔ full. Bring up to 15 lbs. pressure and cook 50 minutes. Reduce pressure gradually; strain and serve as a soup or use as a stock in other dishes.

CHICKEN AND RICE SOUP

Simple, basic, yet inspired.

> 1 plump stewing chicken (2½ to 4 lbs.), cut
>   up as for frying
>   Salt and pepper
> 1 medium-sized onion, chopped
> 1 clove garlic, chopped fine
> 2 tablespoons fat
> ½ cup raw rice
> 1 herb bouquet (2 sprigs parsley, 1 small bay
>   leaf and 1 sprig marjoram or thyme. Tie
>   into cheesecloth bag for easy removal before
>   serving)
> ¼ lb. ham, diced

Sprinkle chicken with the salt and pepper and let stand about 30 minutes. Cook onion and garlic in the fat until onion is delicately browned. Remove onion and garlic and keep. Add chicken to the fat and cook, turning frequently, until it is a nice brown. Transfer chicken to a large pan. Add onion and garlic, rice, 8 cups of boiling water and herb bouquet. Add ham and simmer until the chicken is tender, 2½ to 3½ hours. Take out the chicken, pull off the bones and cut meat into mouth-sized pieces. Put meat back in broth. Check for seasoning. Serve very hot. Makes 6 ample servings.

CHICKEN SOUP—FILLING, FATTENING AND YET DELICATE

1 quart good chicken broth (preferably homemade, at least canned; none of the cubes
will do for this)
1 thick slice onion
1 thick slice lemon
1 lb. chicken breasts
Salt, pepper
1⅓ cups mayonnaise (preferably homemade; not
in any circumstances that which is called
salad dressing)
4 large mushroom caps, sliced thin

Poach the chicken breasts in the chicken stock or broth
with the slice of lemon and onion until the chicken is
blanched and tender. Salt and pepper the stock if necessary. Remove the onion and lemon slice, and place 1
chicken breast in each of 4 warm, large shallow soup
bowls, and keep warm. Let the chicken broth cool slightly.
Stir into the mayonnaise and reheat in the top of a double
boiler. Pour over the chicken breasts and garnish with the
sliced raw mushrooms. Serves 4 very elegantly.

CHICKEN GIBLET SOUP

This soup, delicately thickened the Balkan way with egg
yolks and lemon, is another dish to make with those extra
giblets that have been saved in the refrigerator.

1 quart chicken stock (this may be canned)
3 or 4 sets giblets and necks
1 tablespoon butter
2 egg yolks

Juice of ½ lemon
Salt, pepper

Simmer the giblets and the necks, except for the livers, in
the chicken broth until tender, which should be about 30
to 40 minutes. Remove from the broth and cut up into
small pieces. Strain the broth, slightly cooled by this time,
and add to the egg yolks which have been beaten with the
lemon juice, salt and pepper. Add the chopped giblets and
the livers which have been sautéed separately and diced,
and heat in the top of a double boiler briefly and serve.
Serves 4.

CHICKEN SOUP

In this recipe the chicken is cooked whole and then served
sliced in the tureen with the broth.

1 whole stewing chicken
½ lemon sliced thin
2 onions, with 2 cloves in each
3 leeks, white part only, cut in pieces and very
   well washed
½ cup chopped celery
½ teaspoon thyme
   Salt, pepper
⅓ cup chopped parsley

Put the chicken in a pot with enough water to half cover
the chicken, and bring to a boil. Skim with a lettuce leaf or
paper towel and add the rest of the ingredients, except
parsley. Cover and simmer until tender. Put the chicken
on a warm platter and carve. Add large slices of chicken
to a tureen of the broth, sprinkle with the parsley and
serve a large piece of chicken, with the broth, in every
bowl. This serves 6 generously.

Index

Index